W9-BGI-107

A
Chasing
of the
Wind

Rev. Danny DiAngelo

© 2001 by Rev. Danny Diangelo

A Chasing of the Wind
by Rev. Danny Diangelo

Printed in the United States of America
ISBN 1-931232-13-X

All rights reserved. No part of this publication may be reproduced or transmitted in any form or by any means without written permission of the publisher.

Xulon Press
344 Maple Ave. West, #302
Vienna, VA 22180
703-691-7595
XulonPress.com

Table of Contents

*"Yet when I surveyed all that my hands
had done and what I had toiled to achieve,
everything was meaningless,
a chasing after the wind..."*
—Ecclesiastes 2:11

Foreword

In his book A *Chasing of the Wind*, Rev. Danny DiAngelo speaks from the heart as he shares his very own experience of finding a truly personal relationship with the Lord Jesus Christ. Danny is a man who grew up in church and was steered by others in the direction of full-time ministry. Unfortunately there was one big problem - Danny was preaching to others and yet he did not have a personal relationship with the Lord Jesus Christ. He had religion, but he did not have eternal life!

His story is a living example of how easy it is to talk the talk without walking the walk. I believe that Danny's story is not an isolated case, but that this is actually a common situation in the church and, regrettably, even in the ministry. The fact that you can work a job as a minister and seemingly do it well without having a personal relationship with Jesus is scary, to say the least. Jesus said, "how can you call me 'Lord, Lord' and do not the things that I say?" There will doubtless be many who find themselves in this unfortunate position on the day that they must give an account for their lives.

Danny's story chases a wind, from the pulpit to the night-clubs, and then on down into the depths of self and substance abuse, until 1983, when he had an encounter with God. God dramatically rescued him. He joyfully found Jesus, finally realizing what it means to truly love Him and have an intimate relationship with Him. He also confronted and dealt with the religion and hypocrisy that had almost totally destroyed his life. After Jesus changed his life completely, he and his wife traveled as evangelists until 1991, at which time they pioneered a church in the San Francisco Peninsula, which they still pastor.

I recommend this book as a warning and an eye-opener to those caught up in religion and tradition and also as an encouragement to those who are hurting and disillusioned.

Rodney M. Howard-Browne Th.D., D.Min.,DD
February, 2001

Dedication

To my beautiful wife, Marian, who has been my sole and soul encouragement in the writing of this book. You have enriched my life in ways that cannot be expressed with mere words.

To my son, Santino, and my daughter, Gina, who bring sunshine and laughter into my life every day. You are my inspiration to live the life that I profess.

And, to the memory of the Reverend Floyd W. Thomas, who loved me, as a father loves a son, because he chose to.

Chapter One

A Good Omen

I didn't come from a long line of preachers. As a matter of fact, my father was anything but, unless you count the time that he acted his way through some kind of Elmer Gantry charade in a little Spanish church somewhere in Ensenada, Mexico. Everything was going along fine until his pack of Lucky Strike cigarettes accidentally fell out of his pocket. In his typical fashion, he picked them up and nailed them to the wall with an imaginary hammer proudly proclaiming that "the Lord had helped him quit smoking" and that he had "brought them along to show what the Lord could do."

My mother was incredulous. I guess she really wanted to believe that he had changed and did in fact love the Lord. However it would be what seemed like an eternity before that desire would be fulfilled. Mom could be described as someone who loved the Lord more than anything or anyone else in the world. That made matters worse when it came to her relationship with my dad, Tom.

"How can you live like this, Margaret? You're nothing but a religious fanatic! You're so heavenly minded, you're no earthly good."

And so it went...an endless routine of the battle between good and evil being played out in our little two-bedroom, one-bath house in a quiet neighborhood in San Francisco.

I really can't be too hard on my father. He grew up in an Italian family in upstate New York which was, at best, nominally Catholic. His baptismal certificate said he was christened on September 20, 1914, at Chiesa Italiana di San Giuseppe by Father Angelo Leva. I think that was the first and last time my father went to church.

He was pretty much a jack of all trades and maverick rolled into one. After a brief stint in the Army, stationed at Scofield Barracks in Hawaii, he managed to get transferred to the Presidio in San Francisco due to a foot "injury" received on duty. It took him to Babylon by the Bay just before Pearl Harbor. I guess I should be grateful for the "injury." Just think, I probably wouldn't have been here otherwise. But he did meet my mother there. She was working as an assistant to the dietitian and was a hospitality hostess for the GIs in the Letterman General Hospital. The fireworks were inevitable. The Italian Stallion meets the Puerto Rican Dance Queen.

And so they settled into married life and started a family. My sister, Carol, was born in San Francisco, and a few years later, my father loaded up the Buick and transported his wife and daughter to Chicago, Illinois, where I was born on March 5, 1951. His plan was to make a name for himself in the publishing business as a sales executive. The photograph that I have of him sitting behind a large, wooden desk surrounded by all the trappings of a mover and shaker, including two secretaries, would make one think we had really arrived. He was actually somewhat successful, and Chicago turned out to be not so windy after all.

Just before the migration from San Francisco, Mom made a startling discovery. Life could be summed up in the words of

Solomon; "all is meaningless." It seemed that living out the 1950s version of Good Housekeeping wasn't all it was cracked-up to be.

A husband, a daughter and a home did not fill the void in her life. There was a hunger that could not be satisfied by the mundane pleasures of this world. At the encouragement of some very loving people, Marge began to inquire after the One who could touch the depths of her spirit like no one else. Her own devotion to the Catholic church left her empty...statues didn't speak back...rosary beads just got wet with perspiration in her hands...and the flame of candles eventually died out. There had to be more than religion. In a moment's time during a Pentecostal church service the longing for meaning to life was fulfilled. That was the beginning of her love affair with the Lord.

From that time on, the only thing that mattered was the total surrender of her life to Him who gave His life for her. It was in that spirit that I was conceived.

How wonderful it would be to conceive...maybe a son. I would give him to the Lord. Such were her private thoughts in a moment of closeness to Tom. It wasn't long before those thoughts were realized.

Labor pains led to birth as Dr. Swenson at Swedish Covenant Hospital in Chicago aided in delivery. He was taken aback as the cries of a newborn emitted from within my mother's womb. No need to give me the pat on the bottom...I was already an expert in avoiding a spanking. It wasn't exactly the "voice of one crying in the wilderness," but the kindly missionary physician assured her that it was a good omen.

Now it was time to keep her vow. Following a short stay in the hospital due to jaundice, I was brought to an Assembly of God church in downtown Chicago, pastored by Rev. Devore Walterman. Mom placed her "Samuel" in his strong hands and I was dedicated to the Lord. I suppose my father was there; I don't ever remember him mentioning it. But that's the way our lives went anyway. Mom's life spent in undying devotion to spiritual matters, in which I was included, while Dad pursued a better life for his wife and children, which didn't involve the Lord.

Our stay in Chicago, after I was born, was just as long as my mother's gestation period. So within nine months, the three who left San Francisco returned as four, not counting a Maltese falcon named Joe who made the trip back with us, and occasionally had to run alongside our not-so-trusty Buick while he poured oil into the engine. The oil seemed to run out faster than he could pour it in.

In keeping with my mom's vow, once we settled into a multi-ethnic neighborhood in the outer Mission District of San Francisco, it wasn't long before Glad Tidings Tabernacle became the family church. Well, it was the family church for three out of the four. Mom had attended there before they left for Chicago.

Situated on the corner of a large city block stood the flagship institution of the Assemblies of God. Founded as an independent work in 1912 by Robert and Mary Craig, one-time Free Methodists who had been impacted by the Azusa Revival movement, the Tabernacle quickly became my sanctuary. This was not the run-of-the-mill neighborhood church at the end of a village lane. This was a beacon of light…a spiritual power that emanated from within the bowels of a darkened city—a city of epic proportions, dominated by diabolic denizens that had no use for "holy roller" religion. Into the blackness of spiritual poverty, shone fluorescent letters that bounced off of a massive marquee, jutting out from the front of the tabernacle that proclaimed, with the boldness of an Old Testament prophet, *Services Nightly…2000 free seats…Jesus Saves.*

Glad Tidings wasn't just my sanctuary. It was a haven of rest for the hundreds of San Franciscans who were looking for more than just two hymns, announcements, a twenty-two and half minute homily, and a reassuring benediction that made one feel proud that they had met their religious obligation for the week.

I never ceased to feel that I should be "taking off my sandals" because this was holy ground.

Rather, it was the site of the only real revival that the city had ever known. I never ceased to feel that I should be "taking off my sandals" because this was holy ground. The Glad Tidings Bible Institute had just been moved to the safety of the quiet giant redwoods of Santa Cruz by the time we came to the church. But if you examined the six-story building, built onto the side of the church, that had once housed the students, you could almost hear the intercessory prayers that were prayed into all hours of the night by sold-out lives that would soon cover the globe as pastors, missionaries, evangelists, musicians, and servants of every kind in the kingdom. Walking into the cavernous sanctuary held a treasure of delights for anyone who was among the initiated. As a small boy, I would enter on tiptoe the boiler room of prayer that was built directly under the massive platform, while saints of all nationalities beseeched the Lord for more of the Spirit. Of course, my mother was among the throng. Sometimes it was necessary to break her train of praise and petition in order to get a nickel to put in the Sunday school offering. She would look at me a little bewildered, grant my request, and then again, plunge deep into the Holy of Holies, where her heart knew no bounds.

When I really felt adventurous, my unsandled feet would take me up a flight of stairs that ran alongside the choir loft, through a rich, burgundy velvet curtain, where one would find another flight of winding stairs. On the way up the staircase, I would pass rooms that had at one time been centers of training and impartation for the Bible Institute students. Now they were storage places. There was, however, one cell-like room at the top of the stairs. It measured just about four feet by eight, with little more than enough room to stand up straight in. But you didn't enter that room to stand. Some called it the upper room, but its official name was "The Prayer Tower." Its construction was simple. The only break in the stone wall held a modest-sized, four-pane window; the other wall allowing for a hewn-out altar where the laying down of hundreds of lives to the Lord's will took place. Its only amenities were a dim, unshaded light bulb in the center of the low ceiling and a well-worn floor cushion upon which had rested the knees of those who would be responsible for the preaching of the gospel to untold millions in the years that followed.

Only one person could enter at a time, not just because of the limited space but also because of a hand-painted sign—left on the door from the school era—that made you aware of the one-person-at-a time restriction. I suppose the new school in the suburbs didn't have need of anything so antiquated. The sign still had an awesome effect. Sometimes my young partners in mischief and I would use the tiny room as a secret hiding place, but we could never stay in there very long. I always felt like we had violated God's dwelling place, but I never felt that way when I would venture in alone. It was warm and safe, and I believed that the "prayer closet" had been left intact just for me. I'm glad they left the sign behind.

I suppose the platform held the greatest fascination for me. Behind it was an indented choir loft that was home to a hundred-voice choir. On the far ends of it were abandoned places where a full orchestra had once played the great hymns of the church along with praise choruses full of swing rhythms that one could only hear in a church that had been touched by the fire that had burned through the old livery stable on Azusa street.

But the diamond that reflected the light for me was the pulpit, a honey-colored, oak block of wood that had water stands on each side. Unseen by the congregant was a shelf under that sacred desk where I would view, after the morning service was ended, a hymnbook, a box of tissue, and the ever-present bottle of olive oil for anointing.

That pulpit had not only been Pastor Craig's domain—and now Pastor Key's—but it had also been the sounding board for vessels of clay whose names line the walls of the "Signs and Wonders Hall of Fame." Smith Wigglesworth, Donald Gee, Amy Semple McPherson, Maria Woodworth Etter, W.I. Evans…the list is endless. I had only heard the incredible stories of the miracles that had taken place in that great church. But I was privileged to have seen supernatural power run rampant through that place during many a revival meeting in the '50s. That pulpit was the first place my eyes would land upon entering the sanctuary and the last thing my eyes would see as I left.

"Mommy, when I grow up, I'm going to be a preacher just like Pastor Keys." I was actually two and a half years old when I made that declaration on a Sunday morning while my eyes were glued on my spiritual hero of those years.

I suppose it was inevitable that this earthen pot would stand behind it one day.

Chapter Two

Searching for Shelter

The decade of the 1960s brought political turmoil and social unrest to the nation. It also brought marital turmoil and economic unrest to our home. Whether it was my father's failure to succeed in life or my mother's active church involvement, I'm not sure. Probably a combination of both elements produced an unhealthy situation that my father used as an excuse for an extra-marital affair. I didn't even know what that meant.

All I was aware of was the anguish and heartache that I watched my mother endure. Carole seemed unaffected by the goings on, more than likely because she maintained a close relationship with my father and made allowances for his behavior.

I, conversely, was deeply impacted by the unexpected fissure that broke apart the sanctity of my sheltered life.

"How could you, Tom? Don't you love me anymore?"

"Leave me alone. You'll never understand. You and that lousy church of yours. That's all you think about. I'm tired of living this way, Margaret."

Those seemingly nonviolent arguments eventually escalated into fits of rage and retaliation against accusation. I had never seen my father strike anyone before. I don't even remember being disciplined by him up until that time. Mom was the law, and I had great respect for her commandments. After all, it was she who read the great stories of the Old Testament to me…and books like *Through Gates of Splendor* and *The Shadow of the Almighty*. Somehow, she always answered the questions of my mind…even if the answer was just, "The Lord knows."

Sanctuary was needed. A quiet place away from the storm. I didn't know the wind could blow that hard or that the waves could reach that height. Two places held comfort for me—church and Granny's house.

My grandparents lived a few blocks away from us. The contrast between the two locations was so stark—theirs was a home…ours was a house. Inside Granny's three-story dwelling that I knew so well was harmony. No one in my extended family made me feel like I was loved the way Granny did. I never heard her raise her voice against me even when I spilled an entire box of powdered chocolate all over the kitchen table. As it seeped through the seams of the gray Formica table with the '50s-style chrome legs, I tried furiously to scoop it back into the canister. It was like trying to funnel the ocean into a Dixie cup.

"Ay! Qué bobo," she affectionately mused as she expertly swept the precious granules into the aluminum dust pan. Yes, I had been her clown for a moment, but there was no stinging rebuke, just a warm hug and a trip into the pantry to retrieve another box of chocolate.

Granny's house was a cultural excursion for me. She was the only link I had with the fact that we were Puerto Rican on my mother's side. Her Spanish, not the most educated, had the sound of a tropical breeze wafting through the trees of my heart. Especially when she took her ukulele in hand and began to sing the *coritos* she had learned in a Spanish church in the heart of San

Francisco's Latin district. Mission Bethel was pastored by the wife of my grandfather's first cousin.

This was not the mega-church that I was a part of. This was a one-time Swedish immigrant church sandwiched in between two houses in the middle of the street. Its former inhabitants had moved uptown into a large facility of their own. Josie Lopez sat and clapped her holy hands to the sounds of sizzling steel guitars, hot brass instruments, a stinging bass fiddle and a hundred tambourines being whipped into a frenzy by second-generation Latin Americans who only knew one way to praise the Lord. Singers, full of rice and beans, crooned worship choruses in Spanish, sometimes sprinkling English lyrics into the mixture. Their voices, in lush four-part synchronicity, colored outside the lines of the notes on the pages of music. Only in this church there were no notes on paper. It was all heart and natural talent manu-factured by artisans who could have easily made their living in the nightclubs. Some of them had done just that in the past.

This was church I could get used to. "A Mighty Fortress Is Our God" was not on the play list in this shrine. I watched the musi-cians play into the night and longed to be up there with them. Occasionally, my godfather would motion to me to join him on the platform. He would hand me a guitar, and I would become one with the stream of sound filling the room. It wasn't important that I had no idea how to play the guitar.

After sweat-drenched troubadours and exhausted worshipers were through praising the Lord, Sister Josie would assume her place at the pulpit and launch into a sermon that would take off, soar and land at its destination with the perfection of a trained, seasoned pilot. She didn't know homiletics from hermeneutics. It didn't matter.

Granny's spirituality was as flavorful as her *Arroz con gandules*. Her coffee table held magazines by healing evangelists Oral

Roberts and A. A. Allen, while her record player released the gospel music of Spanish *trios*. In the kitchen, Billy Graham's North Carolina drawl was heard on his radio broadcast, "The Hour of Decision." A safe place for me, indeed!

By the time the emotional upheaval in our house reached fever pitch, Glad Tidings had received a new shepherd. Pastor Floyd W. Thomas, a former missionary to Africa, had taken hold of the helm of a ship that was beginning to feel the effects of urban flight and a changing neighborhood.

Not having a son of his own, he and I "adopted" one another. His strong hands would grasp my shoulder with the assurance that he would not leave me. My father had just vacated the premises. His departure was preceded by physical attacks on my mother. My attempts to defend her were useless, even when I hit him on the head with a blunt instrument. He and his emotions were unscathed.

When Dad refused to take us to church anymore, we would walk to Granny's house to get a ride from my grandfather, whom we affectionately called Nino. One Sunday, while we walked the sleepy blocks, Dad's familiar burgundy sedan came roaring up the street and pulled into an adjacent driveway, cutting off our forward motion.

Thinking he had changed his mind about giving us a ride, Mom and I got into the car. Carole had checked out of church by this time in her life. We sat in familiar surroundings and things seemed to be going well until he passed up the usual exit off of the freeway. The car began to pass through what was, for me, uncharted territory. My mind raced as I traveled farther and farther away from my house and church.

The silence was broken when Tom screamed, "I'm going to kill us all!"

My eyes beheld the orange spires of the Golden Gate Bridge

and as the sedan raced faster, I fastened myself to the floorboard in the back of the car and frantically began to pull out the pages of my Bible.

"Daddy, please stop. Please, Daddy, please."

Almost miraculously, the nightmare was over and we were back in touch with reality. It was too late to go to church now. I sure could have used the strong hands of Pastor Thomas that day.

A year had dragged by. The only reason I was sure of that was because my dad had brought over a few choice Christmas presents. I tried to muster a smile as a gesture of appreciation. It wasn't presents I wanted...but my dad.

School became drudgery and my grades declined. My slight build and admonitions against any type of physical violence made me an easy target for the local bully. I ran to the safety of the Tabernacle. My connection wasn't with the Lord but with the trappings of this great institution and the security it provided me.

Dad finally came home. The affair was over, and just maybe we could resume a "normal" life again. He was back but not changed. His desire to be transformed was evident the night the pastor came to our house to talk with my father. As the exchange between them intensified, Pastor Thomas became increasingly aware that he was not dealing with Tom but with the demons that had plagued his mind and spirit for an untold collection of years.

"Satan, I rebuke you in the name of Jesus Christ. I command you to loose your hold on this man, and I command every demon to leave in Jesus' name. The blood of Jesus Christ is against you."

I sat on the forest green couch in the living room and watched a paroxysm take place as seven demonic spirits were forced to vacate the premises of my father's inmost being. Surprisingly, there was no fear in my heart, just a fascination with the super-natural.

It was as though I could "see" each one leaving and was there to make sure they never came back.

"Daddy, you smell clean," I informed him as he sat down next to me on the couch. He still reeked of cigarette smoke and the lingerings of a battle royal fought on the field of his eternal soul. I was to understand later on that the freshness I discerned was neither organic nor chemical.

His transformation shifted into neutral. In an attempt to reconstruct the family, Dad went to church with us and even took a stab at singing in the choir. I really think he had a secret dream of being another Dean Martin, even kind of resembling him. The perfect picture faded into black and white as Dad lost interest in anything having to do with the church. Now he would wait outside, holding onto a cigarette that had an ash refusing to drop off. I never could figure out how he did that.

Annual missions conventions at the church were a highlight in my life. Due to the size of the ministry and its commitment to the foreign field, we were treated to the best of the best in missionary pioneers. This was back in the days when you could hold a week-long convention and parishioners would actually come out every night.

Each soldier of the good fight would bring his family with him. They would testify, dressed in the native costumes from which they came. Of course, all of them had 35-millimeter film footage of their work in a particular foreign country. Most were from Africa, Asia and Latin America.

The images of natives engaging in pagan rituals, sometimes involving self-mutilation, loomed from the giant screen in the Tabernacle. This was better than the movies. The success of the missionaries' endeavors would be seen as twisted souls were set free by the power of the gospel.

One of the luminaries present during the year that I would

enter my teenage era was a missionary to India. Ovid Dillingham, adorned in a Nehru-style long jacket, had just finished ministering in the Sunday morning service. I wasn't focusing on the content of his message so much as thinking about the vast array of delicacies that would be offered at the Missions Banquet later that afternoon.

"Danny, where in the heck is your mother?" This was my father's usual mantra when I bounded out of the church edifice.

"She's inside talking to someone. I don't know who."

"Well, go get her and tell her to hurry up, 'cause I'm hungry and I want to go home!"

After making a pit stop by the ushers closet in the foyer to retrieve my weekly share of Chocolate Babies from Brother Hartje, the "candy man," I finally found my mother. She was talking to Missionary Dillingham. This was highly unusual for my reticent mom.

"Excuse me, Mom, but Daddy's outside in the car, and he said that he wants to leave right now."

"I'll have to be going, Brother Dillingham. Thank you again for your inspiring message. I will be sure to pray for you and your family."

I was relieved that she hadn't prolonged the conversation. Daddy couldn't be any more cross than before. We were almost making our way up the aisle when Mom said, "Oh, Brother Dillingham, I want you to meet my son."

The elder statesman with silver hair looked at me and gestured to shake my hand. I responded in like fashion, and we exchanged a cordial greeting.

"It is a pleasure to meet you young man. What is your name?"

"Danny," I answered, sure he would never remember our encounter after that day.

"Well, Danny, I..."

His refined speech abruptly became incoherent, at least to my ears. I had heard my mother use this kind of language. Many times after a powerful sermon, someone in the congregation would unleash a flurry of strange sounding syllables that seemed to go on forever. Silence would follow, just for a moment, and then another seasoned linguist would deliver the meaning of what had just preceded in a language everyone else was fluent in.

When he finished speaking in the "tongue of angels," he, still grasping my hand, proceeded to make sense out of what I had been gripped by.

I am going to use you to preach the gospel, and lives will be changed and hearts turned to Me. I will anoint you with My Holy Spirit, and you will be My servant.

"My son, I have called you from your mother's womb. I have set you apart for My glory. I am going to use you to preach the gospel, and lives will be changed and hearts turned to Me. I will anoint you with My Holy Spirit, and you will be My servant. Seek My face and My ways, and I will direct your steps all the days of your life. Thus saith the Lord."

I was merely trying to inform my mother that Dad was getting impatient as usual and attempting to get her into overdrive. That the words I heard were unexpected doesn't cover it well. Was he actually talking to me? Were those words specifically meant to have an impact on my future?

I don't think the missions banquet was ever so delicious as it was that afternoon. Trying to incorporate into my life the verbal mandate I had received was my latest challenge. It was the first time the words "Thus saith the Lord" were spoken over me. Every hint of the call on my life had been either internal or subtle up to that point.

In 1958, Mom had taken me to hear Billy Graham at the Cow Palace in San Francisco. With the rapidity of machine gunfire, the silk-tied evangelist unloaded a barrage of confrontational truth that made the dividing line crystal clear. Either you were a sinner on your way to hell or you were a saint with a home waiting in heaven.

I was neither. I was just an understudy to the man who would have preached the gospel to more people on the face of the earth than anyone else in the annals of human history.

"Just as I am without one plea, but that thy blood was shed for me, and that thou bidst me come to thee, O lamb of God, I come, I come." The choir sang and Dr. Graham gave the invitation.

My eyes were captivated as a sea of humanity made its way to the front of the old cow barn. Just the simple words, "Get out of your seats and come down to the front to accept Jesus Christ," were all he needed to say. I always thought it was kind of him to tell the crowd in the balcony that he would wait for them to get to the front…and then he added that if they had come in a bus, not to worry, because the buses wouldn't leave without them.

Mom was seated next to me, but this time I made no declaration of intent to her. This was a private moment.

"I'll do that someday," I assured myself. Why I would do it was unclear. Was it the power that I witnessed and a desire to soar to that kind of height? Or was it the Lord actually placing a thought in my heart and mind that could never be erased no matter how desperately I might try.

Preaching was a far-off prospect for me anyway. I had discovered my real passion in life: being a drummer. Sometime during

17

my first year of junior high school, I realized an uncanny ability to hear beats and patterns and to imitate them with accuracy far beyond my years or experience.

All other interests took a back seat as I voraciously consumed everything I could get my hands on that revolved around drumming. Magazines, catalogs, browsing around music stores, and hanging out after school in the basement of a seasoned drummer named John Costello became my pastime. John had no interest in Top 40 music. He was a purist all the way.

The KOOL menthol hung from the corner of his mouth as he played himself into a trance-like state, pounding out the big-band sounds of Buddy Rich and Gene Krupa and the jazz classics of twenty years prior. I never knew how old he was, whether or not he went to school, or if he had parents. I just knew he was a great drummer. I don't know if he ever made it out of that basement.

My own drive to be somebody led to the formation a neighborhood band. Another drummer from down the street, the keyboard player, bass player, two vocalists and me on the guitar, that I still didn't know how to play, comprised the next supergroup of the late '60s. Not exactly the Beatles.

For one thing, racially we were anything but homogenous. Four Blacks, a Filipino, and me, an Italian-Puerto Rican or Puerto Rican-Italian (depending on the social setting), made us a sight to behold—especially the first time we debuted. It was a Community Social Fundraiser Banquet. The community was largely Black. The event was held at the Italian-American Social Club. The Irish mayor of San Francisco made an appearance. And, of course, our United Nations band was the featured entertainment. I just happened to be Italian that day.

"Ladies and gentlemen, it gives me great pleasure to introduce our featured guests of the evening...Danny's Band."

How did my father get on stage again? And where did he

concoct that name? I had some explaining to do to the rest of the guys, and I assured them I had nothing to do with the new moniker we had been dubbed with.

Glitches aside, there was a high that came from being on stage, and having the band named after you wasn't too tough to swallow either. And so my passion for music had graduated from the inside of my bedroom to the glamour of being seen and heard by the crowds.

It wasn't long before I had a band at school as well. This time I took my post behind the drums. "The Condors" played at rallies and assemblies, each member of the band enjoying the popularity that being a musician brought with it.

Chapter Three

A Mix of Voices

Balboa High School opened the door to a variety of opportunities. Playing sophomore football and being the sports editor for the school newspaper made up for having to endure the drudgery of scholastic requirements. I wasn't a poor student—it was just that I wasn't terribly motivated. After all, who needed books? I was going to be a star.

Church was no longer an emotional need in my life. School activities and music had soothed the pain in my heart caused by my father. I was still obligated to attend, however, and so decided to make the best of the situation.

Youth Group, with its varied functions, made church life enjoyable. Snow trips, summer camp, and members of the opposite sex proved to be definite reasons for appearing pious.

When Glad Tidings Bible Institute made its move to Santa Cruz, so did the Northern California District Office of the Assemblies of God. District Camp Meetings were held on the grounds of the campus.

By now I was an "old pro" at going to camp. Mom had taken me with her every year since I was a little guy. Granny, my Aunt JoAnne, and Mom and I were regulars on "Cabin Hill." That's where you stayed when income prevented you from higher class accommodations elsewhere on campus.

How anyone could go to services morning, noon, and night was beyond me. But go they did. I could usually con my way into not attending the day meetings, but night services were mandatory.

The up-and-coming musical talent of the denomination was featured in those evening gatherings, as well as the hottest, most fiery evangelists the Assemblies had in its stable. The redwood tabernacle had gone through a metamorphosis as modern seating replaced the hardwood-slat benches, and the sawdust on the floor had disappeared as it made way for concrete flooring. But there was still fire behind the pulpit.

Years of responding to altar calls for numerous attempts to get me "saved" made me an expert at saying what people wanted to hear.

Years of responding to altar calls for numerous attempts to get me "saved" made me an expert at saying what people wanted to hear. Even to the point of mimicking "speaking in tongues." I had heard it all my life. When they could get you to the altar as a teenager, you became a prime candidate for well-meaning, veteran altar workers who were waiting with Pentecostal breath to get you "baptized in the Holy Ghost."

As one saint would lay hands on your head and yell in one ear, "Fill him, Lord," another would place a hand on your shoulder while shouting in your right ear, "Let it out!" As confusion ensued due to the mixed messages, an expert would sidle up on the left and whisper "Hold on" in the other ear.

Desperate to extricate myself from the "charismania," I would rattle off a series of monosyllabic sounds that would satisfy even the most trained "revival meeting ear," and be released out from under the hovering presence of the masters, to the cries of "Praise the Lord. Hallelujah. He's got it."

Having achieved that level of imitation, I would be freed from the clutches of satisfied initiators, released into the night air where I could pursue my real goal, talking to the teenage daughters of pastors who had set aside this week for their own spiritual edification.

I was not like the boys they were used to. Some of them, having come from rural areas of the state with strange-sounding town names like Harmony, Oakley and Chowchilla, had never seen a "city boy." I always used the cultural and sociological differences to my advantage.

The following evening would find me seated in the camp meeting service, surveying the crowd, trying to spy out the young beauty I had met the night before, until the preacher's voice would shatter my concentration.

"Young man, the hand of God is on your life. Surrender to Him, and His will shall be done in and through you. Give Him everything; hold nothing back. Tonight is your night!"

Was he talking to me? Again? This phenomenon had been occurring throughout my teen years from the day that the missionary to India first spoke over me. Why was God doing this to me? What about the other kids I knew? Or any one of the scores of adolescents who were present in those services?

Looking in the direction of the mandate coming from the platform, my eyes would see an index finger pointed in my direction like a heat-seeking missile finding its target. Yes, me again.

Hypocrisy became a way of life for me as I engaged in Friday night "cruising" with my high school buddies. Cigarettes and whatever kind of alcohol we were able to purchase illegally were the fare for the evening. Parties were in abundance, and I made myself no stranger to them. The beginning steps of my walk on the wild side were titillating as I entered places and situations that were sometimes precarious.

"What are you looking at?" The words caught my attention as I realized that a drunken partygoer had singled me out to release his self-generated anger upon.

"Nothing, man," I replied, trying to make a potentially explosive moment casual.

"You think you're cool, punk." As someone else's arms grabbed me from behind, my newly discovered enemy thrust his knee in my solar plexus, dropping me to the floor. A beer bottle shattered, except for its neck, which was positioned threateningly against my jugular.

Seemingly out of nowhere, my buddies appeared, pulling my attacker off of me. We left the party in short order, me showing my gratitude with a simple, "Thanks, man."

While Friday nights were full of adventures in the "kingdom of cool," Sunday evenings found me singing and playing drums in a local gospel choir. Granny's most recent church home, Templo Calvario, was a center of musical activity giving birth to a group of teen and college-aged singers called the Calvary Choir, directed by Fred Cancio.

With no formal training of any kind, the rag tag bunch of choristers would wind their way up and down the state of California, ministering in mostly Pentecostal churches, both in Spanish and English.

Having been introduced to them through my Aunt JoAnne, who was in the choir, I joined them somewhere around my seventeenth birthday. We played churches, revival meetings, conferences and church banquets. I say "played" because to me it was a gig in contrast to a "service."

Amazingly, the presence of God would sweep the room as unpolished voices sang songs of praise and invitation. The services were peppered with the testimonies of choir members who had "found God."

One of the most dramatic testimonies, which always shook even the most hardened sinner to the core, was the story of a local pastor's son named Paul. Rebellious and running away from God, he had left his house one morning on his way to work. As he walked across the street, a car struck him, snagging his arm in the rear bumper and dragging him down the boulevard.

He was pronounced dead on arrival at the nearby hospital. While his distraught mother and sisters shed tears of grief over his sheet-covered body, his still-warm corpse suddenly sat up, the now fallen white drape revealing a very much alive young man.

"Paulie" would hold up a tattered satchel that looked like a magician's case, open it and hold up to the awe-inspired crowd the shredded remains of the very same garments that he had worn the morning of the incident. This was better than magic. He would then proceed to bare his upper arm and show the scar where the chrome "meat hook" of the vehicle had once been lodged, as gasps and cries of unbelief emitted from onlookers who clearly saw that his scar was in the shape of a cross.

A heartrending ballad would be crooned by Fred, embellished with melodic "oohs and aahs" as the service drew to a close. The altar call would be given, and the hungry and sometimes the fearful would cry out to God. The response was always overwhelming.

The devil's playground on the weekend, and God's paradise on Sunday.

Frequently I would be called on to give my "testimony." After all, everybody had to have one. I would begin by introducing myself as a former rock and roll drummer who had seen the error of his ways and "found God." The uniqueness of my story made me a shoo-in for immediate attention after the service was over from the local collection of young ladies present that evening. Life was great. The devil's playground on the weekend, and God's paradise on Sunday.

Mom was pretty much unaware of my worldly activities. I had become proficient at assuring her that I was a good boy, and I still accompanied her to church on Sunday mornings and to an occasional revival meeting now and then. Dad was consumed with his passion for bowling, at which he excelled, so his only concern was whether or not I was safe and had a few dollars in my pocket for emergencies.

One night mom and I attended a meeting in San Jose. An up-and-coming revivalist named Kenn Mann was preaching. We knew he had "the goods," having witnessed first hand, on previous occasions, a bona fide signs and wonders anointing on his ministry. The deaf heard, the lame walked, and seekers were filled with the Holy Spirit in traditional Pentecostal fashion.

The church auditorium was packed...the only available seating being in the rear. Kenn's impeccable taste in clothes caught my attention more than his preaching prowess. The invitation to experience the presence of God was given at the end of his message, and I watched the front of the altar area line with sick bodies and souls four and five deep.

Choosing to stay put, I remained comfortably in the back of the church, away from the hot spot of activity. As the evening wore on, the evidences of the special gifting that operated through Rev. Mann's life were manifold. As things seemed to be winding down, I got out of my seat to go to the restroom, when a by now familiar edict echoed through the loudspeakers. Same words...different voice.

"Son, come here. God has something for you."

"Why me," I queried to the cathedral ceiling. Knowing that I had no other recourse, I made my way down the aisle, stepping over bodies that had been overcome by the power of God. I knew it as being "slain in the Spirit" or "going down under the Power." I had seen it all of my life.

Arriving at the edge of the platform, having ascended a flight of carpeted stairs that wrapped around the circumference of the half-circle stage, I stood face to face with yet another "man of God" who had a word for me.

"You are called from your mother's womb. You have been called to declare the glory of God and preach the gospel. You shall be a vessel for His use. Render to Him all of your life and you will see His plan come to pass. Thus saith God."

Kenn approached me, his right arm stretched out toward the top of my head. My concern was that he might destroy my neatly coifed hairstyle, forcing me to spend the next ten minutes in front of the bathroom mirror.

The instant his hand touched my head I felt a surge of electricity pass through my body, accompanied by a realization that I could no longer keep my body erect.

The instant his hand touched my head I felt a surge of electricity pass through my body, accompanied by a realization that I could no longer keep my body erect. As my frame descended the stairs in reverse order of my ascent, I experienced no anxiety or discomfort. "Coming to" flat on my back on the floor, I was aware that something had happened—I just wasn't sure what the purpose was. That revelation would come later.

High school graduation was approaching and life was going along smoothly. My sister had bought me my first car, a 1956 Plymouth Savoy, two-tone green. The expertly added green sparkle steering wheel gave it panache...especially whenever I made a right turn, at which point the horn would sound. It wasn't the Corvette I had dreamed of, but it was transportation, a necessary accouterment for a senior.

Using the fact that my last name was DiAngelo, obviously Italian, I got a job working at San Francisco's famous Fisherman's Wharf. There I stood in my fluorescent green smock, yelling out the specialties of the day along with the other vendors of shrimp cocktails and cracked crab. What a life.

Life changed drastically as my body began to feel the effects of hepatitis. I had contracted the illness through ingestion of contaminated shellfish. One evening after work, I crawled up the stairs of the house and into my bed. My stay in that bed lasted nearly one month.

Codeine was of no avail, as we quickly discovered, due to an allergic reaction. There seemed to be no cure. I had lost as many pounds as days spent in bed. My jaundiced condition was growing worse by the day. Mom entered my quarantined room one afternoon, waking me from a state of half-sleep. I didn't have the energy or strength to move from that place. It was a shriek that stirred me.

"Danny, your skin is green," Mom cried out. "You looked like you were dead."

The only possibility, according to the doctor, was hospitalization. This wasn't exactly the summer I had planned after graduating from high school. While my buddies were living it up, I was unable to keep anything down.

Being a prayer warrior, my mother laid hold of the "horns of the altar." Her own prayer group, as well as the choir and other Christians, engaged in intercessory prayer for my life. Two weeks later I was out of that bed, totally healed and playing a Sunday night service in Stockton, California with the Calvary Choir.

Summer over, I enrolled at City College of San Francisco, not exactly sure of a major. A school counselor ran me through a battery of aptitude and personality tests to determine my strengths, thereby giving me a better handle on what field of study to pursue.

"Well, Danny, it appears from these test results that you are best suited for a vocation as a social worker, psychologist, or a minister."

"What did you say the last one was?" I asked after the shock wore off.

"A minister," she replied.

Why was God tampering with my existence like this? Being a minister was the last thing in the world on my agenda.

Was this some kind of joke? Why was God tampering with my existence like this? Being a minister was the last thing in the world on my agenda. I chose psychology. No one was going to force me to go into the ministry.

Most of my friends had chosen not to go to City College, some having opted out of higher education and others having selected other venues. Propelled by the boredom that came with scholastics and the fact that JoAnne and some choir members had gone off to school at Bethany Bible College, I followed suit and enrolled at "the place" where all good Assembly of God kids eventually end up. My decision was bolstered by the reality that I was now eligible for the draft. The war in Viet Nam was requiring thousands of young men, and my father was prepared to do anything to keep me out of it. He offered to pay for my Bible College education in order for me to obtain a deferment.

Rain fell in buckets the night I arrived at Bethany Bible College. Armed with a saber length umbrella and clad in a black trench coat that was draped over an Italian made black suit, I made my ascent up three flights of terrazzo stairs, finally reaching the last landing. Each landing of the men's dormitory floors gave way to a lounge area complete with couches and tables for studying or playing the only "religiously acceptable" card game, UNO. There was a great deal of excitement in the air on the last night before classes started the next morning. Feeling a little lost, I approached a few guys who were huddled around a table enjoying the only permitted vice.

"Excuse me, is this the way to the freshmen rooms?"

Assuming that no one had heard me because of the noise level and the fact that my query went unanswered, I repeated the question. One person at the table lifted his head in my direction.

"Listen, we don't want your kind here. Go back to where you came from."

"If you don't want me here, then you're going to have to throw me out!" Was I in Bethany Bible College or in some kind of teenage B movie?

Rising from the table, the former high school wrestling champ made his way toward me to call my bluff. Instinctively, the point of my umbrella found its target, just short of dislodging his Adam's apple. The rest of the "white knights" at the table rose to defend their clansman. He motioned for them to back off, and I eased my way backwards down the hallway to my room. *Welcome to Bible school,* I mused.

This wasn't the first time I had experienced prejudice within the church world. Youth summer camps brought kids from all over Northern California and Nevada. Most of them had never seen and certainly hadn't talked to minorities, especially during the mid-sixties. One particular year, a large group from our church had gone to camp. Blacks, Filipinos, a Virgin Islander, a Hawaiian-Portuguese-Chinese-German-Swedish kid, and me. The summer months would tan my skin golden and make my already curly hair almost kinky when I would perspire from playground activity.

My trained eye had already landed on the long, yellow tresses of a fair-skinned beauty, and I found myself asking her name. I never found out. Her response sent me into culture shock.

"Why don't you go and hang around the other Negro?" she

asked with disgust.

What other Negro? I quickly asked myself. I turned my head to see some of my church friends walking along the thick carpet of grass. Didn't she know the difference between someone from the Virgin Islands and an Italian-Puerto Rican?

Without so much as a glance in her direction, my bronze legs carried me to my cabin where I shed bitter tears of anger and frustration. Yes, I had been down this road before. The uncanny thing was that I had never experienced this in my own church in San Francisco or in a secular setting. Only in suburban and rural religious arenas did I taste this kind of poison.

That year at Bethany proved to be unfruitful as I floundered through my studies, still maintaining that my major was Psychology. Chapel services were boring, and the cafeteria delicacies sent me into town to buy real food.

Unpleasant situations abounded as I witnessed continued racial prejudice toward the only black male on campus. There was never anything blatant or obvious about the treatment James received, but the subtleties were enough to send him into a tailspin of identity loss. The result was terrifying.

Thursday afternoon had arrived like so many others as I sat in my dorm room listening to B.B. King on my record player. Suddenly the sound of what seemed to be a bull moose charging down the hallway was heard outside my door. Running to see what the commotion was, I saw James' massive frame out of the corner of my left eye. He was barely clothed and had just emerged from the men's shower room, where he had struck another student. His head was shaved, along with every trace of facial hair, including his eyebrows. He made a mad dash down the hallway, acknowledging no one. He disappeared out the back door. I never saw James again. Word was that he had been asked to leave the school immediately and had gone back to New York.

Knowing just enough psychology to be dangerous, I was aware that his radical shaving was a sign of emotional disturbance leading to an outburst. Was this the academy of higher spiritual education that had its beginnings in the heart of a multi-cultural city like San Francisco, and whose student body, in those days, reflected the harmonious blend of nationalities and cultures? Without question, things had changed. The bizarre thing was that if you were among the majority, the mere fact of that reality kept you from realizing that the problem existed.

Life was certainly exciting. There was the time that a pack of male defenders of the reputation of one of the campus princesses went on a vigilante hunt to find me, having heard that she and I were out on a date. They were led by the son of a well-known missionary within the denomination, who felt as though it was his mission to teach me a lesson.

Replete with baseball bats and tire irons, the "good old boys" piled into a car and traversed the woods and the beaches of Santa Cruz looking for us. They never found us, but that evening after having already gone to sleep, my room door was forced open. Hands reached into my upper bunk bed and dragged me onto the floor with a thud. My eyes opened and peered out at the leering countenances of the day's pursuers.

Overpowered by the sheer number of them, I fought uselessly as they pulled me down the hallway, descended the stairway, my body scraping against each one of the cruel stone steps. They continued to drag me up the main driveway of the grounds until they reached their final destination.

"One, two, three...." My body was thrown into a pond of water cold enough to send you into hypothermia.

"Are you through?" I asked, as I stood up in rage, intent on getting even. My question was answered nonverbally by a deluge of water coming from an industrial-size garden hose. The proud handler of the hose was the missionary's son.

I made my way back to the dorm, having to pass in front of the girls' dorm, whose residents had been witness to the entire fiasco. Hot water from a shower never felt so comforting.

The intention to get even manifested in a phone call to some of my old buddies at home. The next day, Mickey drove into the parking lot.

"Danny, where are the guys who made trouble for you?"

Dressed in a mafia-style, dark winter coat with a fur collar, he made his way to one of the perpetrators rooms. The door opened, and the person on the other side saw an unexpected and intimidating sight. Mickey's stocky frame was matched by his meanness.

"Listen, jerk. Don't ever mess with my friend Danny again."

The respondent eked out an affirmative grunt as his face was shoved up against the wall by the cigar-like fingers of my buddy.

"I don't want to ever have to come down here again, do you understand, creep?"

Another muffled grunt assured Mickey that any future trips would be unnecessary. And with that he drove back home, having accomplished his mission. No one ever bothered me again.

Chapter Four

Billy Graham and Me

H ey Danny, you have a phone call." The pay phone on the third floor of the dorm could receive incoming calls. I never expected to hear Norman's voice on the other end. Norman was a friend, about five years older than myself, who kind of took me under his wing and showed me the ropes in all kinds of "jungles."

He was a Puerto Rican whose parents were staunch church people in the Spanish Assembly of God in Berkeley, California. The call to ministry rested on him, as well, and he was another runner.

"Hey man, what are you doing this Friday night?"

Thinking that he had another safari planned for us, I responded. "Nothing. What's up?"

"I'm supposed to preach at a youth rally in San Jose...Templo Monte Sinai. I can't make it. I have a date. I already called them and told them you would be preaching instead of me."

"You did what?" Screaming into the phone with a decibel level only heard at rock concerts.

"Don't worry about it, man. You can handle it." His words of encouragement had no effect on my disposition. "Here's the phone number and the directions to the church. Friday night, 7:00 pm. Thanks man. See you later."

I had never really preached, unless you consider the time I stood in our next-door neighbors' yard. I had just turned eight years old and had recently been to the Graham Crusade in the Cow Palace.

The De La Rosa brothers were hanging out of their bedroom windows as I declared the wages of sin and the gift of eternal life while their German Shepherd sat spellbound, fascinated by my gesticulations. My preaching was an amalgam of Pastor Thomas, Billy Graham and Oral Roberts all rolled into one. When the evangelistic crusade came to an anticlimactic close, I bounded over the fence into our yard, bolted up the back stairs and burst into the kitchen, exclaiming to my mother, "Now I know how Billy Graham feels."

That "feeling" was still resident in my soul as I drove my gold Corvair into the parking lot of the Spanish church that Friday night. The car, though still not a Corvette, was a gift from my father who was continuing to make sure that he was "doing right" by his kids.

"Young people, tonight our speaker is from Bethany Bible College. Brother Norman was unable to be here as scheduled because of an emergency."

"Some emergency," I said under my breath as I sat on the platform waiting to assume my place behind the sacred desk.

"So let's welcome Brother Danny." There was a smattering of applause as I approached the pulpit, the youth leader having leaned over to ask me what my last name was, again.

"It's a privilege to be here, tonight," I said, trying to draw on every ounce of data I had stored in my memory bank of preachers extraordinaire. "I want to speak to you from the book of Jonah." Talk about a paradox. Here I was, running from the ministry, telling a church full of teenagers to obey the voice of God in their lives.

The message, which had been manufactured ten minutes before I left for the service that night, came off without a hitch. The ease with which the words flowed from my soul and through my mouth made me uncomfortably aware that this is what I was born to do.

As I gave the invitation for people to commit their lives to God, I watched young Latinos, under the conviction of the Holy Spirit, get out of their seats and find a place of surrender at the altar. I wrestled with myself, feeling the exhilaration of seeing the response to my words and being aware of the sinking feeling in my stomach, as I realized that I had nothing to do with the success of the evening.

Driving back to school, after eating a taco, rice and beans at the pastor's house, I swore I would never preach again, while at the same time, salivating at the prospect of being on the other end of another one of Norman's emergencies.

With the school year nearing an end, I was delighted to toss the application for the next year's enrollment into the trash. I was through with Bible College and ready to enjoy the fast-approaching summer. Needing money to pay for the school loan I had obtained, I found employment at a clothing distribution warehouse in the south of Market district of San Francisco. Glamorous it wasn't, but the pay was adequate.

Still playing drums for the choir and a number of other local gospel groups, a particular Friday night found me at a church in Union City, "gigging" with a hot band for a youth service, when who should show up? Norman.

"Hey man, let's go to San Jose. Andrae Crouch is playing at Faith Temple." Faith Temple was pastored by Rev. Kenny Foreman. The church later built a tremendous structure, and is an ever-expanding ministry called Cathedral of Faith.

I had been there a number of times, having played for various groups like the Calvary Choir and The Latinos. Norman and I flew to the church, arriving just as Andrae Crouch and The Disciples were finishing their last number.

"Oh man, we're too late," I complained to Norman, blaming him for getting us lost on the way.

"It's all right. I know him. Come on, I'll introduce you to him."

Being sure that Norman was fabricating his personal connection with Andrae Crouch and feeling some trepidation, I approached the platform where the gifted songwriter was still seated at the piano. After an exchange of greetings, which made it clear that Andrae actually remembered Norman from a brief time of ministry in Los Angeles at Teen Challenge, the introduction was made.

"Andrae, this is my friend Danny. He's a great drummer." I was grateful for the opportunity to meet him and appreciated the plug.

"Nice to meet you, Danny. You play the drums?"

"Yeah, I play." Was I actually having a conversation with the man whose music I had spent countless hours playing and listening to? How many times had I answered the critics and nay-sayers by telling them that I would play for Andrae Crouch some day?

"Are you good?" Andrae looked straight at me with a seriousness that I knew went beyond musicians' palaver.

How should I answer? If I said yes, my response might appear arrogant. If I tried to appear humble and say I'm just all right, the retort might end the conversation.

"Yeah, I'm good!" My reply was as bold as I had ever been up to that point in my life. Now, I thought to myself, *he probably thinks that this young upstart has a lot of nerve.*

"I'm looking for a new drummer. Would you like to come to Los Angeles and audition for me in a couple of weeks?"

Trying to maintain my "cool," I responded with a casual, "Sure, that would be fine." Inside, my heart was beating out of its cavity.

A couple of weeks later, I heard, "Ladies and gentlemen, we will be landing in just a few minutes at Burbank Airport. Please make sure that you're seat belts are fastened and your seats are in an upright position." These were words that I hoped I would hear again and again.

"Well, let's see what you can do." I sat down at the drums in Billy Thedford's house. Billy, one of the original group members stood with his arms crossed, sporting a well-maintained, large Afro hairstyle. Andrae sat on the couch waiting to see just how "good" this youngster actually was.

The sound system blasted song after song from Andrae's hit album, *Take the Message Everywhere*. With precision accuracy, my hands and feet duplicated the drum patterns I had practiced, ad infinitum, in my own "bedroom studio."

Was it good enough? I didn't dare ask out loud. Waiting for their verdict took every ounce of composure I had.

"You're all right, man," Billy affirmed.

"We have a concert this weekend at a church in Pasadena. Audrey Meier is hosting. Do you want to play?" Andrae, the writer of *The Blood Will Never Lose Its Power*, asked.

Is the sky blue? I thought. "Sure, that would be great."

Is this really happening, I had to ask myself. I was riding in a van with Andrae Crouch and The Disciples, which included former R&B singer, Billy, who had toured with The Johnny Otis Revue; Perry Morgan, a local tenor; and Sherman Andrus, a Johnny Mathis sound-alike whose voice could melt a glacier. Their faces were familiar to me, having seen them on my well-worn copy of their album cover.

"Let's give a warm welcome to our special guests of the evening, Andrae Crouch and The Disciples." The veteran choir leader, Audrey Meier, brought us to the stage to deafening applause.

It was as though I had played with them for years. Andrae navigated the course of music and inspiration, and I watched a master at work. Rhythms, Black gospel piano chords, and soul-stirring four-part harmonies interspersed with ad-lib call and response lead vocals by Andrae and Sherman brought the packed house to its feet, and then finally to its knees.

It couldn't get any better than this. The evening went very well, and I was offered a chance to become a part of a musical entourage that would one day be legendary. Not much thought went into my answer. No soul-searching or petitioning to find the will of the Lord was needed. This was a done deal, a no-brainer. Anyone who would pass up an opportunity like this had to be out of his mind.

With a quick phone call home, I notified my mother of my new life. "Mom, I'm going on the road."

"But what about school...your job. Where will you live?" All were questions that a mother should have asked, and did.

"Don't worry about me. I'll go back to school soon, and I really don't like my job anyway. As far as where I'm going to live, Andrae said it would be okay to stay in his house." Things were handled, and with an obligatory call to my boss, I was no longer part of the working class. I was a professional musician, playing for the hottest contemporary gospel music group in the country.

Unfortunately, I became a legend in my own mind.

We traveled from city to city, playing the largest churches and concert halls on the West Coast. I flew home to San Francisco when we had some time off and, of course, was a big deal among the hometown folks. Someone from among the ranks had made it. Unfortunately, I became a legend in my own mind.

Dad was always there, however, to assure me that I was larger than life. Picking me up from the airport was a source of pride for him. He would take me immediately to his place of work, just a couple of miles away, parade me around the plant, announcing to all of his cronies, "This is my son Danny. I just picked him up from the airport. He's a professional drummer, you know. Plays for Andrae Crouch . . . flies all over the place."

I think my father was living his life, vicariously, through me. He possessed great style and could have actually been much more in life if he'd had the chance. Growing up in New York state as one of nine children of Italian immigrants and having dropped out of school in the eighth grade didn't exactly provide for success. He had numerous career failures and never really found his niche in life.

I always thought that deep down he concealed the dream of being an attorney. When he didn't bowl anymore, except for an occasional game or two, he would, on his day off, get dressed to the nines, usually in a gray and black, hounds-tooth, two-button suit, a crisp white shirt and a burgundy tie with a matching pocket square.

No date, nor any business appointment—just an afternoon spent at the local courthouse watching the Perry Masons in action, fantasizing that he too had passed the bar. He would report to me, with great amusement, how individuals he passed in the hallway, would ask him if he was trying a case that day.

Shortly after I became a "Disciple," we took off on a whirlwind tour of the world. Hong Kong, Tokyo, Saigon, Bangkok, London,

Edinburgh and Jakarta were sites that served to expand Andrae's ministry, and I was overwhelmed to be a part of it. While most eighteen year olds were in exotic places because of the military, I was experiencing the thrill of a lifetime because I played the drums.

Arrogance and youth is a deadly combination. The events that resulted from that unwise decision took years to overcome and resolve.

When the three-month-long tour ended in Hawaii, I left the band because of a relationship in Los Angeles. Arrogance and youth is a deadly combination. The events that resulted from that unwise decision took years to overcome and resolve.

Returning to San Francisco was less than rewarding. Having spent seven months on the road with Andrae was pretty hard to beat. I yearned to be back on the big stages, flying in airplanes and receiving my share of the attention that went along with being part of the group.

Settling for playing with the choir again and working in a men's clothing store was getting monotonous. Because of my reputation as a former Disciple, I did one-nighters with a slew of local and regional gospel groups whenever the opportunity arose. But these things did not satisfy my thirst or my ego.

The summer brought with it Camp Meeting, and it seemed like a good excuse to get away from the boredom I was tolerating. Mom had already been there for four days, and I drove up to visit her and hear the latest "find" in the Assemblies of God.

Danny playing with Andraé Crouch.

Danny playing with Andraé Crouch in Indonesia

Danny playing with Andraé Crouch in Indonesia

During the evening meeting, District Superintendent Rev. Joe Gerhart announced the speaker as the foremost evangelist of the proud denomination. Marvin Schmidt preached like a Jeremiah with a fire in his bones. The "signs and wonders" side of his ministry had more impact than any I had ever witnessed before.

Sitting with Mom and Granny in the bulging auditorium—fourth row from the front…right hand side, just where they sat every year—I watched the Rev. Schmidt operate in virtually all of the gifts of the Spirit as recorded in I Corinthians 12. To say that I was impressed is an understatement.

The service was winding down as my mind maneuvered the impending ride home through the Santa Cruz mountains, when my mental charting was interrupted by the voice of the evangelist.

"Young man, come up here! Yes, you."

O.K. How many times does this add up to? I had almost made it out the door without incident. I was sure this time would be uneventful. Fat chance!

Standing opposite Marvin, approximately eight feet away, he spoke words I had heard over and over since the first time in 1963. There was an embellishment this time, however.

"May the prayers of this young man's mother and grandmother be answered. Son, you are called of God to preach the gospel of Jesus Christ, and your life can never belong to anyone else but Him."

There was no conceivable way for him to be privy to the incense of intercession that had been burned on the altars of my mother and grandmother's hearts. As the reality of the preceding moment rushed through my psyche, the words, "Receive the anointing" floated above my conscious mind. A soft wind brushed my face, and my body fell backwards with a thud on the platform. I didn't see Rev. Schmidt blow air out of his mouth in my direction, having had my eyes tightly shut as I pondered the words that the voice of God declared through his servant. You can't see wind, but you can see its power.

The ninety-minute drive home that evening left me plenty of time for introspection and meditation. Shelving the experience of that night into a "to be handled later" compartment brought me back to the mundane and uneventful, or so I thought.

One afternoon in 1970 the phone rang. I was getting ready to go to work convincing portly men that they looked fantastic in the latest designs from Europe. The voice on the other end was familiar, and I immediately recognized it as Sherman Andrus's.

"Hey man, we're in Oakland. We have a concert tonight at the Oakland Auditorium with Dallas Holm and David Wilkerson. Andrae wants you to play. Can you make it?"

Like the trigger of a gun releasing a cocked hammer, I went into motion. First, a phone call to my boss to tell him I wouldn't be able to come in to work, followed by a trip to pick up my drums from the rehearsal studio that the choir rented.

Dallas Holm opened the evening and we followed, setting the stage for David Wilkerson, whom I had met earlier in the evening. I was back in business. It felt great to rub shoulders with the who's who of the Christian world again.

All good things come to an end, was the thought that hovered over my emotions as we made our way to my house to drop me off. After a time of fellowship around the kitchen table, Andrae asked, "Do you want to go back on the road?"

The fact that my employer had called during the evening and informed my Dad that my services were no longer necessary, coupled with the choir leader's call on the heels of my boss's call, letting me know that I didn't need to make the next service because I had skipped a rehearsal to play with Andrae, led me to say a quick "Yes."

After all, who needed a minimum wage job working for a Mussolini with a Napoleon complex and playing for a local group of weekend warriors? I was back in the "big time."

Bags packed and drums in the van, we rolled out the next morning on our way to Portland, Oregon and Seattle, Washington. Two weeks later, we headed back to Southern California to play numerous concerts over the following months.

I was living with Perry Morgan and his family this time around. Sherman Andrus was entertaining the idea of going it on his own. We had become close friends, rooming together almost everywhere we went, and when he asked me if I wanted to form a new group with him, the only thing that needed to be done was get my "stuff" and move it into his place.

Having played with a couple of local musicians from the East Bay for a number of years, I assured Sherman that these were the guys we needed to add to the group. We took a trip back home and recruited a quiet bass player named Carlos Ramos and a mischievous guitar player named David Botello.

These were excellent musicians who had never gotten the exposure they deserved. They were so unexposed to the big picture that their naiveté manifested in hilarious ways. Sherman had driven back to Los Angeles and the "Burrito Brothers" and I flew to meet him a couple of days later.

During the flight, David announced that he was hungry. The minuscule bag of salted peanuts wasn't "hitting the spot." Without hesitation, Carlos reached under his seat, retrieving his "suitcase," a bowling bag containing his worldly goods. Reaching down into his version of a Pierre Cardin travel bag, he pulled out a circular package wrapped in tin foil.

My eyes stayed glued on his activity as I tried to imagine what the contraband cargo was. Peeling back the carefully secured wrapper, he lifted out a powdery white, homemade, flour tortilla the size of a truck tire, and without a second thought, he handed it across the aisle to David, while corporate executives in Brooks Brothers suits watched in disbelief.

Suddenly the flight attendant was standing in the middle of the transfer, at which point Carlos looked up at her with shiny olive-black eyes and graciously asked, "Would you like one?"

And so began a new series of adventures as "The Brethren" was birthed. Within a few weeks, a veteran keyboard virtuoso was added to the group. Ike Jones had played for gospel greats such as The Caravans and worked with a successful R&B conglomeration called "The Watts 103rd Street Rhythm Band." Finally we ran into a recent Bible School graduate from the San Fernando Valley who wanted to be "in the ministry." Lacking any discernible music skills, he was put to work as a roadie and sound technician. His platinum hair forced us to dub him "Towhead."

Our bookings, guided by the expert care of Dick White, a former talent agent for such names as Diana Ross and Jerry Beaven, a one-time associate to Billy Graham, we did our share of touring throughout the state of California and the Southwest. We worked throughout the state of Texas, playing anywhere from little Mexican missions on the other side of the tracks to the prestigious First Baptist Church in Dallas, pastored by Dr. Criswell.

In between were sandwiched television and radio appearances, state fairs and college dates, such as Hardin-Simmons College and Baylor University, where we met a behemoth who actually consumed nineteen hamburgers before our eyes. One week found us in Tijuana, Mexico, where we were the musical guests for a citywide evangelistic crusade with Luis Palau.

Our popularity was increasing, and there was talk of a TV pilot in the offing, in the same vein of The Monkees sit-com. One sweltering weekend took us to San Diego to be part of a USO show at Camp Pendleton. Sitting on the military transport bus with a variety of entertainment has-beens, a character who looked like he had stepped out of the pages of a Mickey Spillane novel approached me.

"Hey kid, are you an actor?" The gray smoke from his Cuban cigar made my eyes smart.

"Yeah, I'm an actor." I responded, having nothing to lose.

"What have you done?"

"I've done a few walk-ons and some summer stock," I replied, thankful that I had watched enough Tonight Show interviews in the past to sound like I knew the ropes.

Asking me if I had an agent, he informed me that I was perfect for a part in a soon-to-be-produced film called "The Godfather." My eyes quickly perused the contents of his business card that he handed me, *Paramount Studios...Albert S. Ruddy, Producer.* The stranger's name was somewhere on the card, but that item was irrelevant.

Instructing me to call him to set up a screen test as soon as I got back to Los Angeles, he walked back to his seat, a stream of Havana exhaust fumes in his wake. Fingering the card, I assured myself that I would do just that, but there was a gnawing notion in the pit of my stomach that prophesied ultimate destruction should I pursue it. The card went into my chest of drawers and disappeared among its contents.

Chapter Five

No Safe Places

Almost as suddenly as "The Brethren" began, it disintegrated. Carlos, the tortilla-wielding ace bass player, announced that he was going back to college. Ike headed out for greener pastures, and Towhead left to pursue a love interest.

It didn't take an expert in ancient languages to read the handwriting on the wall. David and I floundered in Los Angeles for another couple of months and finally took our last plane ride together. Sherman was drafted by the well-known southern quartet, "The Imperials," and became the first and last Black member the group has ever had.

The Calvary Choir was still as faithful to their calling as ever, and it seemed natural for me to fall back into the slot I had made for myself. This time I brought David and Carlos with me.

A once thriving Youth for Christ and Campus Life ministry in San Francisco during the 1950s had now become just a memory. A longtime supporter of the work was a member at Glad Tidings where I was still attending in order to please my mother.

With a desire to renew the work, he asked me if I would start Campus Life clubs in the local high schools and produce YFC rallies once a month. It seemed like another golden opportunity to become "somebody," and I jumped at the chance and plunged headlong into the work.

Within a few months, a couple of hundred high school kids were filling a local auditorium under the resurrected banner of Youth for Christ. While the success of YFC was a given on the national level, even the relatively small number in attendance in a city like San Francisco reflected great progress.

Summer break was upon us, making the operation of the clubs nearly impossible, in spite of good intentions. That, compounded by a lack of financial and moral support from the local clergy made YFC, once again, a shadow of the church community's past.

During the last few days of closing down the operation, the telephone rang in my room one evening. Thinking that the days of the "big break calls" were no more, I answered it with little interest. The usual greeting was countered by a familiar voice.

"Danny, this is Nicky."

There was only one Nicky that I knew whose molasses-thick, New York-Puerto Rican accent immediately identified him as the main character in the best-selling book, *The Cross and The Switchblade*.

There was only one Nicky that I knew whose molasses-thick, New York-Puerto Rican accent immediately identified him as the main character in the best-selling book, *The Cross and The Switchblade*.

Nicky Cruz's path and mine had crossed a number of times,

first through my old mentor, Norman, and then in different venues, where either he was speaking or I was on the road with any one of a number of gospel music groups.

"Wha' are ju doing?" One needed the gift of interpretation of tongues to be able to understand Nicky completely.

After a brief rundown of my recent activities including the collapse of the ministry of YFC, he told me to meet him at his hotel room at San Francisco Airport. Twenty-five minutes later, Nicky and I were knee-deep in "road stories," peppered with Latin humor and a supply of hot coffee that sustained our laughter into the night.

The evening's hilarity was interrupted by a question that nearly floored me. "How would you like to be my associate evangelist?"

Could this be one more chance to grab the proverbial brass ring? Nicky's ministry had widened well beyond the first time I had heard him in a Spanish church in Oakland, California. He was internationlly known and respected, his gift as a soul-saving herald of the gospel placed him in great demand while he filled auditoriums across the country and around the world.

"When do I start?" The old southern colloquialism, "My Momma didn't raise no fool," was my mantra.

With the same speed that I had employed in taking advantage of numerous other chances to get back on the road, I packed my bags and jumped on a plane to Raleigh, North Carolina, where Nicky's ministry headquarters were located.

This time, however, I didn't fly solo. Realizing the potential danger of being a young evangelist traveling alone, and at Nicky's subtle urging, I married the girl I had been dating for almost a year.

Nicky and I traveled together as I "opened" meetings for him, as well as preaching in local churches as an advance man, to stir the interest of a religious community where he would be conducting an upcoming crusade.

My involvement in the ministry was expanding as opportunities for me to speak were increasing. One such opportunity arose as Nicky held a weekend rally in Akron, Ohio, at the Cathedral of Tomorrow, pastored by the veteran of Christian broadcasting, Rev. Rex Humbard.

I sat next to the man whose face I had seen on television a hundred times, while preparing to introduce Nicky. As I lifted out of the ornate platform chair, Dr. Humbard put his hand on my shoulder with the instruction, "Get up there and give your testimony, boy."

Not wanting to disobey the hero of the faith and being cognizant that my function was to promote the books and tapes for sale and set the stage for Nicky's ministry, I delivered a brief, re-hashed account of the former rock and roll drummer who found Jesus. The crowd, seated under the huge lighting structure in the form of a cross, seemed moved by the story. It was everything I could do to pry my finger loose from the edges of that pulpit. But, of course, this was not my night. After the service, an usher handed me a note from a parishioner who wanted to let me know how much my testimony had impacted her life. How ironic it was that my "story" had an impact on people, but had none on me.

The weight of the burgeoning ministry brought Nicky to a point of exhaustion. He took a sabbatical and went to Puerto Rico with his family. In the meantime, my responsibilities were almost nil, and Nicky sent me to Fayetteville, a nearby city, to work as Public Relations Director for Outreach for Youth, the rehabilitation facility for boys that was under the umbrella of his ministry organization.

Arriving at Fayetteville's city limits, I was met by a massive billboard. The color scheme was fire-engine red and white with coal-black letters. Absolutely sure that the sign's message was some sort of telling joke on the past, I turned to the executive director of the boy's home, who had driven me there, and remarked that the billboard must get a lot of attention.

The red background hosted a large drawing of a white-hooded man, riding a white horse, holding a burning cross in his hand. The onyx letters screamed as a mandate,

Fight Communism and Integration. Support the Ku Klux Klan. Welcome to Fayetteville.

He shattered my misconception when he assured me that this was not a joke.

This city was the ultimate in culture shock. In-your-face racism and Sunday Blue Laws that forced the town to virtually shut down during church hours, plus a restaurant selection that offered only one Mexican food establishment whose delicacies tasted like Taco Bell Lunchables in the freezer section of a super-market.

Part of my job was to introduce and generate interest in the ministry within the community. Reaching into my music background, I formed a "choir" out of the residents of the home, utilizing the success stories of former addicts who had been set free from the bondage of drugs and alcohol, and began a tour of the local service organizations.

The Rotary, The Lions, The Elks, The Moose Lodge (and any other kind of benevolent group with animal names that I could find) were a natural choice for telling our story and an opportunity to solicit financial support.

Churches were also open to the ministry and many a Sunday night was spent taking my troupe into some of the bastions of Southern-Anglo religious fundamentalism. These were the times that opened the doors for me to preach. The ministry enjoyed a measure of success, and my speaking schedule began to get crowded. I had no complaints, except...

Not traveling and working directly with Nicky proved disappointing. Part of the reason that I had joined the ministry team was because of my relationship with him. The organization was undergoing a major revision, influenced by the board of directors, offering a "golden parachute" to anyone who wanted to bail out. Taking advantage of the situation, I returned home to San Francisco during Christmas of 1974.

Donna, my parents' surprise package, was now seven years old. A year had passed since I had seen her, and she had grown so much during that time. Not much else had changed, however, especially my marital relationship. I had realized soon after the wedding ceremony that I had gotten married for all the wrong reasons. The "union that wasn't "continued to be fruitless in every way.

The bond that had existed between Pastor Thomas and myself was still very much intact. A place was made for me on staff at Glad Tidings, at first part-time while I continued my education in Philosophy at City College, and then full-time as Youth Pastor when the position opened up.

Pastor Thomas took me to the District Office of the Assemblies of God and made arrangements for my Youth Ministries Licensure. The jumping through of hoops was nominal given the fact that he was the General Presbyter of the district. My father's adage was true, "It pays to know people."

Three years of babysitting, snow retreats, summer camps, youth choir and dealing with adolescent behavior was beginning to take its toll on me and on a crumbling marriage. September of 1976 held a devastating moment.

The church secretary buzzed my office with the usual communiqué. "Danny, line two is for you."

Answering without any hesitation, I heard a voice that had

been like my own breath all of my life. The sound of it was unsettlingly altered though.

"Danny...Daddy's dead." Carol's sense of emotional self-control was still her strength.

"Come now...we're at the hospital."

My fingers had lost all power to grasp the receiver as it crashed to the desktop in my office. The Tabernacle wasn't safe anymore.

Dad had suffered for a number of years with stomach pain, especially after dinner. Despite constant admonitions to see a physician, he was bull-headed and refused to take anyone's advice. Two years prior to that fateful month of September, he had, in desperation, finally sought medical help.

It was two years too late. He had been diagnosed with colon cancer. Operations and treatments had little or no effect on the all-consuming pestilence from hell. Emaciated and filled with fear, my father laid in the bed during one of the horrific stays in the hospital.

Oddly enough he had turned on the television and was watching Rex Humbard on a Sunday morning. Lulu Roman, the former Hee Haw star, was giving her testimony of how the Lord had delivered her from a life of drug abuse and self-degradation.

Tom's heart of stone began to soften as she sang of the Lord's love and grace. When Pastor Rex had finished his simple message, Dad opened his heart to the truth that sets men free. My mother's prayers had finally come to fruition.

The last two years of his life were spent in and out of the hospital but never without suffering. If someone had told me when I was a child that I would one day have to carry my father—now an 82 pound sack of bones draped with skin—in my arms to the bathroom and administer an enema, I would have told them they were crazy.

I was just there last night. This doesn't make sense. He seemed to be resting peacefully when I left him. He can't be dead, this is just a bad dream.

My mind raced as fast as my 260Z as I flew low to the ground on the way to St. Luke's Hospital. *I was just there last night. This doesn't make sense. He seemed to be resting peacefully when I left him. He can't be dead, this is just a bad dream.*

Dad's condition had declined to the point of his being unable to speak. Before leaving his room the night before, I had held his tired hand and told him that I had forgiven him for all of the pain and turmoil of the past and that I dearly loved him. With a gentle squeeze, he let me know that my sentiments had reached into his heart. A string of tears ran down the side of his now sunken face, and I placed the last kiss on his forehead.

Crashing through the double doors of the hospital, I frantically entered the all too familiar elevator to arrive at his room. Mom, Carole, my Dad's sister, Rose, and her husband, Arnold, were standing in their places of grief. I opened the room door and saw my father's lifeless body, eyelids still open.

Running to the nurses' station, my voice demanded "Who was with my father when he died? Why didn't you try and revive him? You let him die!"

They assured me that all measures had been taken and proper procedures had been followed. He had expired due to complications as one of the nurses was taking his vitals. My venting over, I gently made my way into the place of total sorrow and sat by his side, placing my head on his chest.

The sound of fluid in his lungs gurgled out of the open hole in his face that once was used to express his love for me. Anguish, in liquid drops, flowed from my eyes as I realized my protector was gone.

How many times had he given his last dollar to provide for me? Even my first set of drums had been purchased with the money from a settlement he had received from a work-related injury. His constant concern was expressed in the words, "Do you have money?" as he placed a hard-earned twenty in my hand when I would leave for a night out. It was his way of showing that he cared.

It was as though I recognized my responsibility and assumed it, instructing the family to leave. Everything would be handled. Dad would have wanted it to be so. Sitting in the room, watching his motionless frame, I relived the good and the bad, occasionally verbalizing my thoughts, as though he could hear me. Four hours later, the orderlies entered the room to begin the routine of preparing the corpse for transfer to the mortuary.

"You'll need to leave, sir," I was instructed.

"Please allow me to stay. I'm a minister. I'll be fine."

My gaze beheld every move they made as Dad's body was turned on its side, his back facing me, revealing bluish-purple epidermis, where his blood had sought it own level.

The final closure was made as his face was shrouded with the peach-colored butcher paper, as though he was just another slab of meat for delivery. No, he was my dad.

Comfort was nowhere to be found. All of the funeral arrangements rested on my shoulders. During the service, I read a poem I had written in memory of my father. The last line read *"So this is not goodbye, it's just see you in a little while."* However, I had no assurance that I would go to the place where his spirit had flown the moment he died.

The ability to endure my own hypocrisy was wearing thin. The charade had come to an end.

The ability to endure my own hypocrisy was wearing thin. The charade had come to an end. A few months after my father's death, I resigned from the church staff, standing on that awesome platform that had been holy ground to my feet all of my life, and informed the congregation that God was "leading me in a new direction."

I couldn't very well tell them that I was a phony…that I had no relationship with God…that I had simply been an actor in a stage play that had had its final performance. The "show" closed along with everything else. Within a matter of weeks, the curtain was brought down on the marriage. I vacated the theater, and looked for a place to find myself.

Chapter Six

The Wind Howls in Spanish

Where do you go when the only place you feel comfortable in is the church? What language do you speak in a foreign country known in the church as "the world"? Having been trained all my life to do the "work of God" left me clueless as to the path my feet should trod.

Realizing that the ability to persuade and convince had been a strong suit, it seemed only natural that my father's old profession was something doable for me.

A friend of Carol's owned a number of small businesses and needed a salesman to generate a client list. Finding a small apartment close to his shop, I was ready to pursue a career in big business. The big business was me sitting in a dusty little room with a telephone and a business directory, trying to solicit accounts for a janitorial service. This was not the prestigious life of Madison Avenue advertising I had imagined.

Getting tired of having the phone slammed in my ear and a thousand "no thank you's" a day, I decided to get away for a while. With a few dollars in my pocket and a car that could run like a thoroughbred, I drove down the coast of California, stopping in Oxnard, a little town near Ventura.

The Rolon family was glad to see me. We had become acquainted over the years during my travels in gospel music. Rev. Robert Rolon was a pastor and always made room for itinerant ministries.

"*Muchacho, como estás?*" It sounded like music to hear Sister Rolon's Puerto Rican-flavored Spanish. "Get your things out of the car. You're staying with us for as long as you want."

One didn't argue with Becky. One just obeyed. I was relieved to find a safe haven and enjoyed the incredible hospitality of these wonderful people.

Sunday morning was hectic as the five members of the family prepared to go to church. Robert came into my room, "*Mira*, I want you to preach this morning."

Not having divulged all the details of my life, it was only natural that he would feel free to ask me to speak. Well, one more performance wouldn't matter. The gift was still there, as people responded to the appeal to open their hearts to the will of God.

One evening during my stay, a dream sequence appeared on the wide-screen of my subconscious. I was in a darkened hallway lined with closed doors on either side. Searching the corridor, my hand opened one door after the other. The places, people, and events of my life were displayed in vivid imagery, sequentially, in every room that I peered into. It was as though my search for reality was contained in this venue. In a state of exhaustion, after running from door to door, dripping with perspiration, I collapsed in front of the last doorway. A dim light cast a yellow shadow on the handle. Reaching up to grasp the knob, I told myself that behind this door was my answer, my future, the reality I was looking for...

The door creaked open and swung wide, disappearing behind

the supporting wall. A sickening odor permeated the atmosphere of obscurity. Lifting my head to see the shadowy figure standing over me, I viewed the shrouded form of what appeared to be a man. His arms were crossed and his facial features were contorted in a look of cynicism and smug pride. He spoke to me.

"What did you think you'd find behind this door? God? You fool...you're going to serve me. Ha, ha, ha..."

His sardonic laughter trailed off as my conscious mind began to take control of the moment. The sheets of the guest bed were soaked with terror. Calming myself with the reassurance that it was only a dream, I finally drifted off back to sleep singing the refrain, "It was only a dream, only a dream..." Or was it?

Feeling like I had overstayed my welcome, my journey continued to Southern California where I visited the existing members of the Disciples and sat in on a studio recording of gospel great Jesse Dixon. L.A. held nothing for me now.

Back in San Francisco, I was determined not to try to reenact "Death of a Salesman" and went to work in a small women's shoe boutique on what was known as The Miracle Mile, in the heart of the Latin district.

While there, the publisher of City Magazine came in to do some business with the owner. Not finding him in, the visitor struck up a conversation with me. Twenty minutes later, I was an account executive for one of the city's best-known publications.

After a year of honing my craft and doing some modeling in conjunction with the display ads the magazine produced, I was convinced that I was ready for "bigger and better."

A day of scouting through the yellow pages landed me an interview with the sales manager of the top pop music radio station in the city. He didn't have any openings, but believing I would be an asset to any sales team, he referred me to a Spanish language radio station in San Francisco. An hour later, I was "in radio."

With music still very much a part of my life, I began playing congas with various jazz and Top 40 bands in the area on weekends. Life had changed drastically from the days at the Tabernacle. My appearance had more of an entertainment flair, long curly hair, a close-cropped sculpted beard, a virtually unnoticeable diamond stud earring in the right ear, designer clothing and the ever-constant European cigarette in my mouth. Definitely not the look of a former minister.

Being single and determined never to become involved with anyone as long as I lived, both my profession and weekend activities in music provided a myriad of opportunities to enjoy my singleness.

Radio was paradise. Working in media sales brought financial as well as emotional rewards. Expense accounts and complimentary tickets to almost any entertainment activity in town made the simplicity of the church world seem like tasteless pabulum. Nothing could make me ever darken the doorway of a church again.

My sales ability had opened up avenues for revenue in the larger advertising agencies that had not previously considered Spanish media as a wise investment and had decided against making them a part of their yearly budget. Large national accounts started to be heard on the station's airplay, and my contribution to the successful turn of events did not go without notice.

Coca-Cola was interested in the young Latin market and agreed to sponsor a weekend music package geared toward that group. The onset of "disco" music was reaching every culture and was a natural music source for a bilingual and bicultural show. The three-hour package would be rounded out with dance music, originally from the islands of Puerto Rico, Cuba, and the Dominican Republic, then funneled through the sieve of first and second generation musicians in New York and Miami. The music was known as *Salsa*.

Since there was no one working at the station who was familiar with both music styles or anyone who had the ability to host the bilingual show, the current sales manager asked me to do it. I never refused the chance to shoot for the moon, and the following Saturday evening at 9:00 p.m., car radios and home stereos blasted with the hottest Latin and Disco music of the moment as Coca-Cola-sponsored *Saturday Night Salsa with Danny DiAngelo*.

The popularity of the program seemed to reach never-anticipated heights, almost overnight. The management was thrilled and the sponsor was happy, but neither was as ecstatic as the host.

Out of total obscurity, my name and visage became synonymous with the hip Latin sound of San Francisco.

Out of total obscurity, my name and visage became synonymous with the hip Latin sound of San Francisco. Print ads using my picture for product promotion and a life-sized color picture in the front window of the Mission District's most frequented photography studio added to my notoriety. The huge "promo pix" was shot as part of a promotional campaign for a South American beer company. *Listen to Saturday Night Salsa with Danny DiAngelo. He drinks Brahma Beer.* Not exactly the kind of testimonial my mother had hoped for, but that wasn't important. The only thing that mattered was that I was becoming "somebody." The picture stayed in the store window on Mission Street for two years at the owner's insistence. She maintained that it was great for business.

The show's impact on the community and my career began to expand into new dimensions. Local concert promoters saw me as a natural for emceeing shows. The biggest names in Salsa music were being imported from the Caribbean as well as New York and Miami, where significant enclaves of Puerto Ricans and Cubans, respectively, were located.

Thousands of young adults, bilingual and bicultural Latinos, whose ancestors had come from every country representing Latin America's diversity, were thronging to venues like UC Berkeley's Greek Theatre, the Cow Palace, the Oakland Auditorium, the Circle Star Theatre, Convention Centers of the Bay Area, and sold-out ballrooms in the posh hotels of San Francisco.

Excitement and the latest in high fashion were the order of the evening. No jeans and tee shirts in this venue. The "stars" of Latin music displayed their wares onstage while dance and concerts goers gyrated in synchronized fluidity, imitating the traditional dance forms of their ancestors from their beginnings in the islands and countries of origin. Dance couples who made Astaire & Rogers look like they were standing still filled the floors of the Bay Area as *Salsa* spiced-up the night.

My role was to make sure that the different bands were ready to take the stage on cue and prepare the frenzied crowds for the next act.

"Damas y Caballeros, Ladies and Gentlemen, are you ready to party? My name is Danny DiAngelo from Saturday Night Salsa. Now put your hands together and welcome, direct from..."

Any one of a large number of artists' names and places would fill in the rest of the line. Each one having a particular handle or nickname that they were known by, the addition of which added more punch to the introduction. The more the intro was embel-

Danny with Celia Cruz, legendary Salsa artist from Cuba.

Danny with Ray Baretto, Latin band leader and recording artist.

Danny with Tim Reid, "Venus Flytrap" of the television show WKRP in Cincinnati.

lished, the higher the expectation level was for the crowd.

Levels of expectation weren't the only things that were high. Drugs and alcohol seemed to be a part of the package that went along with the lifestyle. While on a break between introducing bands, I slipped into the restroom of the concert hall. A smartly dressed, young man approached me and told me he enjoyed my radio program. We exchanged pleasantries as I watched him pull a small folded bindle from his inside jacket pocket.

Unfolding it with the greatest of ease and care, he retrieved a miniature silver spoon from his navy blue gabardine pants pocket, scooping out a tiny spoonful of the white powder that was held in the package in his hand. Raising the tool to his right nostril, he expertly inhaled the contents into his nasal cavity and proceeded to follow the same pattern with the left side of his nose. His dark eyes watered, looking like he had taken an unexpected bite of horseradish.

"*Bendito*, that's good stuff. You want a hit?"

"Sure. *Grácias*."

I wasn't sure what it was he had ingested nor did I have any idea of what the effect would be on my physical and psychological person. It didn't matter. I was intent on taking in everything this kind of life had to offer.

It had been an incredible journey from the afternoon that I sat in the raised section of the Cow Palace with my seven-year old eyes glued on Billy Graham. Here I was, having just left the same stage in the same place, twenty-two years later. That moment in 1958 when my inmost being decreed that I would "do that someday," no one could have known that the only similarity between that moment and this one would be the place itself.

I'd always had the knack of imitating what I saw, and now I repeated the procedure I had just seen. The inward blast of my nostrils released a stream of fire as the cocaine rushed through my nasal passages and into the rest of my system. My eyes glazed as the same biting effect of the white substance stung my sinuses.

Minutes later, the euphoria of the drug was released. A sense of pseudo-empowerment swept over my psyche accompanied by a total abandonment of the guidelines and parameters that had been my regimen for the majority of my life.

"Man, you were right. That is good."

I gave my approval to his proffering as though I were a seasoned connoisseur of the highest quality product of Colombia's narcotic business. His gracious offer of another "hit" was thankfully taken, as I prepared myself to bring on the next act.

The radio program had developed a significant listenership and a wise nightspot owner in San Francisco's Embarcadero Center approached me with the idea of doing my show live from his supper club/night club as a remote broadcast on the radio station.

At nine o'clock p.m. the familiar theme music and intro line blared from the station's transmitter through radio speakers and into the hearing of the Bay Area's Latin audience.

"You're tuned to Saturday Night Salsa with Danny DiAngelo, tonight coming to you live from La Fuente, in the heart of the Embarcadero Center of the City."

Within a span of one hour, the place was packed with party-goers, to the delight of the club owner. Complaints from local merchants found their way to the top of the tower where the nightclub was located, due to the traffic jam on the street caused by soon-to-be patrons, waiting to get into the parking lot under the building. La Fuente was a smash hit and became the place to see and be seen every Saturday night. We expanded to include Friday evening as well—not on the air, just using me to DJ as a drawing card to fill the place.

The number of guys with little white packages in their suit pockets who wanted to "hang out" with the DJ seemed to grow every weekend. Having enjoyed the effects of the drug, and being tired from working the weekends in addition to my regular weekday sales position at the station, I never turned down an invitation to a concealed spot to get "high."

My Bible, only read out of the necessity to prepare a sermon, was now buried in a box along with the vestiges of an ex-preacher's life.

My life had gone through a metamorphosis, and nearly all traces of my former existence had vanished. My father was gone, the church would never be a part of my routine again, old friends and companions were a memory. My Bible, only read out of the necessity to prepare a sermon, was now buried in a box along with the vestiges of an ex-preacher's life.

In their place was an extensive music collection of Salsa and disco music, cartons of European cigarettes, imported Russian vodka, and complimentary bindles of cocaine given by small-time drug dealers.

Two people were significantly important in my life. My long-time friend, Carlos Ramos, had joined the radio station sales department and was sharing a two-bedroom Victorian flat with me in the city's Mission Dolores district. Always wanting to share my successes with him, I turned over the Friday night DJ activity at La Fuente to him. He was now enjoying the popularity that went along with being "somebody." He, however, never seemed to need it the way I did.

Carlos and I were brothers in a way that most people rarely have the privilege to experience. Much like the David and Jonathan friendship in the Old Testament, he and I watched out for one another, sacrificed, and willingly gave whatever was needed to each other. Surrounding our closeness was a cast of characters that had become a part of my inner circle by means of the radio station and the nightclub.

Now, having been promoted to the position of General Sales Manager of the radio station, my circle of influence widened in the community along with my relationships.

Maintaining an iron will to avoid emotional commitments to women, my romantic interests amounted to nothing more than flirtatious encounters and conquests as numerous and varied as the proverbial "fish in the sea."

The word "surprised" hardly describes my reaction as the other person of significance entered my life. A typical evening at La Fuente always closed with me sitting on a barstool waving a casual "goodbye" to the patrons. Complete with a smoke in one hand and a "Stoly" in the other, my eyes took in the sights of the female patrons with the experience and expertise of a veteran jeweler appraising the value of fine diamonds. This night there was one jewel that shined more brilliantly than any other I had ever seen.

Chapter Seven

Another Soldier Goes Home

Long, raven-colored hair caught the corner of my eye. Turning my head to get a good look at the owner of the tresses, my eyes took in all of Marian's beauty with one head-to-toe sweep.

She had come to the nightspot with her sisters and some friends to have dinner and remained for the evening's festivities. I begged with a motion of my finger for her to come to where I was seated on my favorite barstool. Exercising caution and a wise skepticism, she gingerly made her way over to me, saying a fairly cordial "Hello," followed by a polite question about what I wanted.

Doing my best to engage her in conversation, I started with the usual routine of name, age, where are you from and what do you do questions. After I managed to assure her that I was not a "bad guy," no matter what she might have heard, she reluctantly gave me her phone number after I had asked twice. I definitely made use of it.

Pursuing a relationship with her, which had been strictly taboo for me, I found that she was a college student studying music. Probing a little further, she brought up the fact that she was a pianist and vocalist in a Spanish Southern Baptist church in the city. The church girl was nearly floored when I told her that I had played with Andrae Crouch and had been an associate evangelist to Nicky Cruz. She wasn't impressed, just in a state of unbelief.

Virtually no one knew who I had been in the past. My rise to local celebrity had taken place like a phoenix out of the ashes. Most people in the community simply assumed I was a transplant from the East Coast. No one would have ever imagined the truth.

Finding it increasingly difficult to consider Marian as just one more in a string of meaningless flings, I took our dates seriously, making room for her in my very neat, compartmentalized life that had until now barred the doors to any intrusion of serious romance. She continued her studies and decided to pursue a career in the medical field. Having aptitude and youth on her side, being twenty…and nine years my junior, she had no problem in realizing her goals. Her sheltered upbringing put her in sharp contrast to my man-about-town image.

My only goal still remained the pursuit of significance. The radio station continued to provide for my basic needs as well as my involvement in entertainment. The weekends were jammed with dee-jaying at La Fuente, emceeing shows and spending time with Marian.

The hectic schedule proved tiring, making cocaine my drug of choice due to its effect on the nervous system. Any fatigue or sense of depression was immediately, though temporarily, eradicated with the ingestion of a "few lines."

The majority of people I knew and associated with had access to the white powder. Because of my status, there was never a lack of people willing to get me "high" for free. There was the expectation of a favor, however. Backstage passes to concerts and names on my guest lists were part of the exchange. There really isn't any such thing as a "free lunch."

Working a show or keeping a dance floor full of dancers that looked like marionettes in motion, connected to a set of invisible hands became a task as the months rolled by. Cocaine or "blow," as it was called, was the battery acid that kept everyone's motor running. At times, the engine would misfire.

"*Damas y Caballeros, welcome to the Rathskeller. Tonight's guest is the one and only Ray Baretto*...." My usual banter done with, I retreated to the bathroom to rendezvous with a pair of local drug dealers who had been my guests that evening, coming to hear one of the veteran conga players of Salsa and Latin Jazz and his orchestra.

"*Con cuidado, Chacho*," Jimmy cautioned, as my nose filled with the latest sampling of goods from Latin America. Looking at my watch reminded me that the band's set was almost over and it was time to go back to work on stage.

The corridor from the men's room to the ballroom started to spin in circular motion. My legs turned to lead weights while my perspiring palms left trails of sweat as I groped for the walls so as not to fall on my face. The urge to vomit was so intense that my only thought was to get to a private place so I wouldn't make a spectacle of myself.

Managing to turn a doorknob, an otherwise mundane task that had now become Herculean, I stumbled into an unused banquet room, falling face down onto a serving table. In the distance, the last riffs of Ray's break tune passed through the back of my head, telling me I had to get to the stage.

My body had weathered the toll that cocaine takes many times before. But my heart had never thumped this hard or this fast. The sweat oozed from every pore while my clenched teeth held back the river of bile mixed with Remy Martin coming up from my stomach. The red glow of the exit sign above the double doors of the room came and went as I passed in and out of consciousness. I was overdosing.

"Danny, Danny. Can you hear me? Somebody call an ambulance. He's dying."

"Danny, Danny. Can you hear me? Somebody call an ambulance. He's dying."

Members of Ray's band tried to revive me. They had gone looking for me when I missed the curtain call. Coherent enough to assure them I wasn't dead, I told them to cancel the emergency call and just help me back to the bathroom. Once inside, with some help, my appearance was put back to as close to normal as possible.

Soon I was back to schmoozing with the audience as though the preceding events had never taken place. After bringing the band back on, it was back to the same place for a little more.

The world I lived in had no church ghosts from the past to haunt it. Any images from the hallowed halls of holiness were a distant memory. However, a telephone call from my mother brought the two spheres together.

"Son, I knew you would want to know about Pastor Thomas."

I had lost touch with him over the last few years. He was the only person I really missed from the past. To the denominational hierarchy, I was just another statistic of those who had resigned, on the inside back page of the monthly ministers' magazine.

"Danny, he has cancer and is in the hospital. It doesn't look like he's going to be here much longer. I know you'd like to see him."

Approaching the private room of my "church dad," I greeted his three daughters. The youngest, who was a couple of years older than me, had been a member of my exploring team as we rummaged through the ancient porticos and alcoves of the Tabernacle as children.

Sister Thomas opened the thick hospital room door and motioned for me to enter, seeming genuinely happy to see me again. She graciously left the room so "the man" and I could have a private moment. Sitting on the edge of his bed, his steel blue eyes brightened as he recognized me.

The strength to speak eluded him as he lay there trying to let me know that he welcomed my visit. Tragically, this was not the first time I had seen this kind of scenario.

"Hi Pastor. It sure has been a long time."

His eyes blinked in an affirmative code. Grabbing his hand in mine, I pried open the bars of my heart.

"I'm sure you know all about me now. That's not why I'm here. I don't know if I'll ever see you again. But I came to tell you that you have meant more to me than any other man I have ever known, other than my father."

His once strong hand gripped mine with a strength that seemed to have returned just for me.

"I want you to know that I will never forget you. You will always live in my heart. I love you very much."

Leaning forward, I kissed his forehead knowing that this was the last time I would ever have the opportunity to do so. The eyes that had watched over me since I was eight years old were now pools of tears, expressing everything that his mouth was unable to say.

Standing in the back corner of Glad Tidings Tabernacle, clad in black attire and black sunglasses, my gaze was fixed on the mahogany casket centered just below the pulpit that had been

Pastor Thomas' private domain for over twenty years.

Longtime associates and ministry peers filled the platform chairs, having come to lay accolades of honor upon the memory of the fallen soldier. As each one testified to the character and faith of the man who had once braved the jungles of Africa during the early 1950s, those who had come to pay tribute nodded their heads and said "Amen" in the filled-to-capacity sanctuary.

I yearned to tell them how wonderful he had been to me, of the wise counsel he had freely given to me on many occasions, the sumptuous lunches that we enjoyed so many times. He knew the best restaurants in San Francisco and had taken me to almost all of them. I wanted to inform the crowd of just how unique he was. I felt as though I had been privileged to see facets of his personality that no one else had.

With great affection and respect, I had always called him "Boss," during the years I served under him. No one knew that his eyes would twinkle whenever I told him that he was the Godfather of the Northern California/Nevada District of the Assemblies of God. No one knew these things about him. I wanted to run to the pulpit and let them know just how incredibly wonderful he was. But ex-preachers don't get that kind of privilege.

Another opportunity to achieve greatness crossed my path in the form of a pair of nightclub owners. I had signed on with the rival Spanish station in the city and was continuing to enjoy the same popularity I had relished with the former station. Meanwhile, an unlikely duo of entrepreneurs approached me with a tantalizing offer.

They owned a well-situated nightspot in the outer Mission District that had enjoyed a string of successes over the years, transitioning from one era and culture to another. As far as they were concerned, it was time to tap into the Latin market. What better pipeline to young, hip, bicultural Hispanics could there be to make this happen than me?

Expectant partygoers lined the sidewalk, while giant search-lights scanned the night-sky, signaling an invitation to the city's newest mecca for Salsa and Disco. Inside, the darkness, perme-ated only by wall sconces and disco lights, swallowed every patron in its atmosphere. The custom-built stage in the corner of the room held the instruments of the hottest Salsa bands in the Bay Area.

Situated within full view of every eye in the place was the DJ stage, replete with key lights focused on the persona I had created.

"Ladies and gentlemen, you are at Casanova's, San Francisco's premier Latin Nightclub."

Outside, those still waiting to get in stood under a Goliath-sized marquee, featuring the silhouette of an elegant couple dancing.

The club quickly became the place for the elite of the city's Spanish community to gather. A strict dress code kept out the undesirables and guaranteed that only the most fashionable were afforded an entrée. The latter also included drug dealers.

Casanova's, a name that I was proud of having given it, was an after-hours club, making it one of the few legal places to continue to party throughout the night. Anyone wanting to make a "connection" off the street knew that the popular venue would have any number of small-time hustlers waiting to ply their trade.

This was yet another venture that Carlos Ramos and I were involved in together. He took care of the night's receipts and was responsible for the bar operation, cocktail waitresses and bounc-ers.

My responsibility as host was to book the bands and make sure, as usual, that the music and the party never stopped. There was always a steady stream of "helpers" who made sure that I never "came down."

The back office was where I would retreat from the congestion of the packed house, frequently accompanied by a designer suit-clad dealer. Young Latinos who had decided to take the easy road to fast money poured hundreds of dollars of cocaine onto a large mirror laid flat on my desk, their expensive jewelry reflecting off of the glass as they lined up streaks of the "gas" that kept the motor running.

The satiation of my hunger for power and satisfaction was finally being realized. Money was no problem, dining in the best restaurants the city had to offer was routine, the much sought after drug of choice for the crowd I ran with was just a gesture away and, most important of all, Danny DiAngelo was a force to be reckoned with.

Cocaine use not only gives a feeling of euphoria, but it also contributes to a false sense of self-confidence and feelings of independence. The popularity of the new endeavor and the monetary rewards that accompanied it convinced me that I didn't need to continue to work in media anymore. All of my energies were focused in one direction: making Casanova's the epitome of a New York City style nightclub with all the trimmings.

There were moments when the hustle of the Friday night through Sunday morning madness would resolve into periods of introspection and the pondering of my existence and fate.

One such weekend ended with a drive down the coast of California to spend a couple of days with an old friend. Leon Patillo had walked into the sanctuary of Glad Tidings on a Sunday morning while I was the youth pastor there.

To say that he looked out of place would be the height of understatement. While the majority of the parishioners attended church in "Sunday go to meeting" clothes, Leon entered dressed in a purple velvet suit with silver piping around the lapels and pockets, purple patent leather platform boots adorned with metallic silver stars, long hair and a goatee. Not exactly church board material.

His entry caused quite a stir, and Pastor Thomas's knowing glance at me was my assignment to check him out after the service. After a standard introduction, we engaged in a series of questions revealing his profession. He was a musician. This was somebody I could relate to.

Leon was the lead singer and keyboard player for the world famous group, *Santana*. I couldn't help but ask what in the world he was doing in the bastion of Pentecostalism on a Sunday morning.

To my surprise, he acknowledged that he had given his life to God just five days prior, having been guided by his girlfriend's brother who happened to be a Christian. Needing to find a church, he chose one in close proximity to his house, ending up at Glad Tidings.

Leon and I clicked and began a friendship that lasted through the years of ministry and into the era in which I was now living.

Leon and I clicked and began a friendship that lasted through the years of ministry and into the era in which I was now living. The uncanny thing is that while I was in the church, we spent a year's worth of days together when he was off the road, during which I would disciple and counsel him in the things of God.

The paradoxical nature of that relationship went beyond

bizarre. The uninitiated initiating the learner...the blind leading one who had just received his sight. Leon reached a place of no return in his walk with God, making the decision to leave the Grammy award-winning music icon and strike out on his own in the Christian market.

Not having any connection to the gospel music world, he was wondering how he would be able to make any inroads into the field. I had become acquainted with a burgeoning youth ministry in Sacramento called The Warehouse and was able to book Leon into his first opportunity to be exposed to the Christian Contemporary Music arena. That single booking led to a record contract with Marantha Music.

His career took off like a shot as each record album gained greater acclaim, making him a concert draw across the country. We worked a couple of concerts in town during those early days of his ministry, Carlos and I playing for him.

"Leon, I don't know where I'm going or what I'm doing." I settled into the lush chocolate leather couch in his octagon-shaped refuge set in the woods of Santa Cruz. "When the music stops and the "coke" is gone, I'm alone, and I wonder what life is really all about. As emotionally and physically satisfying as my life is, there's a gnawing feeling in the pit of my existence that won't go away. The only thing that makes any sense is the relationship I have with Marian and the few friends that I can really count on."

A couple of days later, as I was just starting down the winding road from his house on my way back home, Leon sat down at the piano and wrote the Dove Award-nominated song, I *Surrender*, my encounter with him having been its inspiration.

Almighty God, Savior of my soul
Cleanse me today and make me whole
So here is my life. Take complete control
I surrender, I surrender
All that I am to you, my Lord
Lord, let your Spirit fall on me
I need your direction so desperately
'Cause most of all I want to be
What you've created me to be
I surrender, I surrender
All that I am to you, my Lord
Sometimes it's hard to give all to thee
But here I am Lord, on my bended knee
For the highest place on earth is still at your feet
I surrender, I surrender
All that I am to you, my Lord

The fulfillment of those prophetic words was a long way off.

Chapter Eight

Does the Wind Exist?

ruising Mission Street in a red Excalibur convertible had a way of taking one's mind off of the complexities of life. My "bosses" owned a fleet of collector cars, any of which I had access to for my personal pleasure.

Immersed back into the duties of managing Casanova's, the weekly routine left little time for self-examination. The cycle of prosperity seemed, however, to be going off kilter, spinning out of control.

Another overdose, this time in my office, sent a clear message. This roller coaster ride may not come to a complete and safe stop, allowing the rider to push forward the safety bar and exit to the right.

The success of Casanova's had negatively affected the revenue of the other Latin nightclubs in the area. The rumor that a contract had been placed on my head was, to my ears, nothing more than someone's idea of a bad joke.

A normal Friday evening found Carlos and me making preparation to open the club for the evening. It was usually his job to go to one of the owners' home to pick up the money for the weekend's operation. This weekend Carlos was involved in a project, and it was up to me to make the run.

Opening the front door of the club, out of the corner of my eye, I caught sight of a plastic bag. Upon investigation, I realized the content of the bag was gasoline. Not paying much attention to the "intruder," I told one of the bartenders to come and get rid of it.

Five feet from where the bag of potential danger had been, my car was parked under the giant marquee. Getting into my RX7, I happened to look down, finding another gas bag carefully positioned under the driver's side of the car. My attention now fully focused, my usual routine of tossing out my cigarette onto the street before I took off seemed unwise. Shaking off the unsettling thought of the obvious with a line of cocaine, I picked up the money and made my way back to the club. This night of surprises had just begun.

"Pull the car over."

No, not the voice of a squad car's loudspeaker, but a strangely reassuring sound coming from somewhere in my hearing. The voice repeated the command as the smoky gray sports car came to a standstill in front of a large building a mile away from my original destination.

"Get out of the car and go inside the building," the still quiet voice instructed.

Wanting to play this scenario out to its completion, I found myself walking into a beautifully ornate Catholic church. Once inside and realizing that the lights were on but nobody was home, I turned to leave, thinking that the drugs had really begun to take their toll on me. Voices telling me to go into a Catholic church? Had I paid too many visits to the theater of the mind?

Just as I reached the exit, thinking I would make a hasty retreat into reality again, I spied a row of what looked like closets above which there were red and green indicator lights of some kind.

Assuming that these were what the Catholics called confession-als (my knowledge of the Catholic Church having come from seeing too many Bing Crosby movies in which he played a priest), my curiosity got the better of me, and I took an investigative expedition of the little rooms.

Realizing that green meant go and red meant stop, I stood in the darkness of one of the closets after the "green light door" had shut. My hands unsuccessfully explored the walls for a light switch. Finding none, my feet searched for some kind of floor button that would turn on the lights. My search was interrupted by the opening of a small, screened window. The welcome light from the other side enabled me to see my hands again.

"Bless you, my son."

The voice came from a partially visible face, with a nose that protruded like the boot of Italy and a mouth seen only in profile.

Not having been raised Catholic, never having been in a confessional, and not knowing anything more than the fact that Catholic school kids had a lot of holidays that public school kids didn't have (a fact I had learned growing up next to the De La Rosa family), I was at a complete loss as to how I should respond correctly.

"Yeah, bless you too."

Although I found out later that the appropriate reply should have been the acknowledgement of having sinned and the asking of the priest's blessing, I answered in the only way that made any sense to my Pentecostal upbringing.

The priest, obviously aware that I was not a "confessional professional," asked the purpose of my visit. My response was to relate to him, in short order, the events of my life. Coming to the end of my "confession" I made a declaration of desperation:

"I don't know if God exists. I don't know anything about all the things I was taught and what I preached. I only know that if there is a God, if He's real, I have to find Him."

"I don't know if God exists. I don't know anything about all the things I was taught and what I preached. I only know that if there is a God, if He's real, I have to find Him."

Being raised in evangelicalism, I grew up hearing the normal banter of a seeker's testimony that would always include a reference to having "found the Lord." Hence, the need to "find" Him was a reasonable mission statement.

The wise priest's response fell on my ears and struck against the formula I had come to think of as the way things were supposed to work. "Son, when you're ready, God will find you."

The radical nature of that message staggered my mind. To think that somehow there was a moment in time predetermined by God when the searching of my soul might come to an end and that He was waiting in the wings to reveal himself to me was more than I could grasp.

Exiting in a state of confusion, I retreated to the refuge of Casanova's and took up where I had left off, the last words of the clergyman echoing in my ears, overpowering the high decibel volume of the music.

The strangeness of that night was to continue. Two different factions were enjoying the revelry of the evening. One, a Puerto Rican drug dealer and his entourage and the other, a Cuban rival who was in fierce competition for the same market share.

Things went along as usual until it was time to close. After seeing out the last patron, Carlos bolted the black doors and went to count the money. I was in the middle of shutting down the sound system when I heard screams followed by what sounded like a car backfiring twice.

Running to the bolted doors that were being desperately pounded on, I reached inside my velvet jacket to make sure my small caliber pistol was within reach. Carlos and I quickly opened the doors just enough for two young ladies who had been in the club that evening to enter and escape the gunfire.

The rival contingencies had faced off directly in front of the club's facade, people scattering in every direction when the guns were drawn. The two girls, now safe inside, had managed to extricate themselves from the line of fire. However, an innocent victim, one of the band members, did not escape the melee and lay on the sidewalk, blood soaking his white tuxedo shirt from the two holes in his abdomen. The shots, fortunately not fatal, did paint a picture of violence associated with the club throughout the community.

I was in the middle of shutting down the sound system when I heard screams followed by what sounded like a car backfiring twice.

The darkness that seemed to hover over the now well-known venue, showed no signs of decreasing. Violence permeated the atmosphere, compounded by the large amount of drugs ingested inside the club by its patrons as well as its management.

San Francisco's finest made regular visits due to Casanova's reputation. Whenever the midnight blue uniforms hit the door, their gold badges bouncing a reflection from the strobe lights, anyone who had something to hide would make a dash to the bathroom or my office, if they had privileged access, to dispose of or hide their wares.

One particular Saturday night brought them to us, this time by invitation. Manny, one of the bouncers, had approached me on stage during a set change. His tropical dark skin now looked ashen.

"Someone just called and said a bomb is going to explode in five minutes. We need to get everyone out quickly and without hysteria." Manny's chilling message sent me into protection mode.

"Call the cops and tell them to get here with a bomb squad, now! I'll get everyone moving in smooth fashion and Carlos will secure the building."

To our relief, the call was a hoax. However, a recently hired bartender confessed that a local club owner, by whom he was formerly employed, was responsible for the call and the gasoline "bombs."

When the cycle of destruction begins spinning, it carries with it a velocity that sweeps along every manner of debris. It was in that context that a middleman in the chain of command of a Colombian drug cartel approached me.

Small in stature, the white-suited Central American, who was a frequent and big spending patron, asked to talk with me privately. After sampling his wares in my office, I was offered the opportunity to be a part of the operation by allowing use of the club as a "money laundering" front.

All I had to do was process the gross revenues from the cocaine business through the weekly receipts from the club, show a profit and loss balance, the hidden difference going back to the middle man, and take my percentage for my "trouble."

Life had brought me to a place of bravado so intense that there wasn't much of anything that I was afraid of.

How could a one-time Pentecostal preacher become part of a drug operation without even the slightest apprehension or twinge of guilt? Life had brought me to a place of bravado so intense that there wasn't much of anything that I was afraid of. Nor was there the sense of wrongdoing in my soul. After all, I was just some guy trying to grab hold of some kind of reality that satisfied the screams for significance in my spirit.

"I'll be back in two weeks for your answer, Danny," he said as he drove off in his "fresh off the lot" BMW.

The following two weeks flew by while I pondered the prospect of big money made the easy way. Telling no one about the proposition, I waited for some indication of what I should do. At times it seemed like the solution to all of my problems, and other moments of pondering led me to see it as the possible beginning of a nightmare.

The loud knock on the front door of my two-bedroom, Victorian flat echoed down the hallway into my bedroom. "Who's at my door at ten o'clock on a Thursday evening?" I asked myself, making sure to grab my shotgun on the way to the door.

"Who's there," I called, with a sense of paranoia.

"It's me. Leon. Open the door. I have to talk to you."

It had been a couple of years since Leon and I had seen each other. Quickly ushering him inside the living room after putting the rifle safely away, I insisted on knowing what had brought him to my door completely out of the blue.

"I was praying for you, man. The Lord told me to come and tell you that whatever it is you're about to do...you're chasing ashes."

"What do you mean? Who have you been talking to?"

I was sure that he had gotten an inside line on my proposed business dealings. But then, on the other hand, no one knew about it. How could he have known anything?

"I don't know what it means. I just know that the Lord told me to tell you that you're chasing ashes. That's it. I gotta roll. Later, Brother Buzz."

And with that he slid into his gold Mercedes and was gone into the night.

Dumbfounded doesn't even begin to describe what I was feeling or thinking. There was no way for him to have had even the slightest inkling of what was going on. The uncanny events of that evening led me to decide against getting into "the business." Strangely enough, six months later the entire ring was busted, and everyone involved ended up in federal prison.

Had I found myself yet? Did my search for significance have a gratifying end?

For the first time in six years, since the day that I walked out of the church, I stepped off of the "people mover of life" long enough to watch the madness from the outside looking in. *Had I found myself yet? Did my search for significance have a gratifying end?*

My life seemed like the lyrics to a song:

Are we really happy here, in this lonely game we play?
Looking for words to say.
Searching but not finding understanding anyway.
We're lost in a masquerade.

The things that I thought would bring true satisfaction were only a temporary panacea for a disease that had ravaged my soul. The popularity I enjoyed, the lifestyle and the feeling that I was accountable to no one was countered by the drug overdoses, the botched attempts on my life, the loneliness that would over-whelm me at times, and the knowing that there was a gaping hole inside that nothing could fill.

The only constant was my relationship with Marian, which by this time had become more serious than any I had allowed over the last six years. The theme song of my life was interrupted one evening by a phone call.

"Danny, would you go to church with me tomorrow night?" Mom knew better than to ask me a question like that. Had she forgotten the conversation we had just a couple of months before?

"Mom, just forget about me ever being in church again. I'll never be in the pulpit again as long as I live. Let the vision die! It's a pipe dream and it will never, ever happen. I have no use for the church or anything connected to it. Do yourself a big favor and pray for something else."

For the next three weeks, following that conversation, my mother was heartsick. The truth of Proverbs 13:12 was borne out in her experience, "Hope deferred makes the heart sick, but a longing fulfilled is a tree of life." Her joy and zeal for her God seemed to have dissipated until she stood on the unshakable promises of God that "He who has begun a good work in you will perform it."

Standing on the promises, she continued her invitation. "Rev. Paul Schoch is holding meetings at the church. Why don't you go with me? If you go with me this time, I'll never ask you to go again."

This was an offer I couldn't refuse. Enduring one simple church service with an evangelist I had heard numerous times before during my church days would be the guarantee that would insure that Mom would never ask me to go to church again.

Chapter Nine

Caught Up in the Wind

The telephone startled me from a deep sleep I had fallen into. "Hello," I managed to mumble, dragging the receiver to my ear.

"Danny, this is Donna. Are you asleep? Ooh, Mom is going to be mad if you don't go to church. You better get up and get ready."

My baby sister, now sixteen years old, scolded me into the shower.

Marian and I were originally supposed to go out that evening, but she encouraged me to go to the church service.

"Oh well, it's too late to change my plans anyway. Besides, after I do the hour and fifteen at church, it'll be just the right time to stop in at one of my favorite haunts on the way home."

Getting dressed to go to Glad Tidings now seemed foreign to me. With the exception of a phantom-like appearance at Pastor Thomas' funeral, I hadn't been back in six years. Nor had I run into anyone from the old Tabernacle during those days. I suppose everyone just assumed that I had gone the "way of all flesh" and wrote me off along with the rest of the once-shining lights that had now faded.

Arriving fashionably late, my eyes drank in the honey-colored walls of the foyer that had served as a place to play hide and seek when I was a child. Easing through one of the four sets of double doors, I sauntered down the seemingly mile-long aisle way.

A murmur went through the crowd of worshipers as they caught sight of the once-familiar profile of a little boy who had grown up in front of them and had once served them.

Spotting my mother's shining white hair, I stationed myself at the end of the pew, next to her, for a quick getaway. It looked as though that escape route was going to be necessary soon enough.

The congregants were lifting hymns of the faith combined with modern-day praise and worship choruses that seemed like relics from an ancient past to me, and my discomfort was evident in my demeanor.

Standing among the mostly conservative crowd gathered that evening, my attire was definitely out of place. The black leather trench coat made the diamond stud in my ear lobe appear all the more brilliant in contrast.

The usual worship service preliminaries, now safely out of the way, were followed by the introduction of the evening's speaker. Paul Schoch was a consummate veteran of decades of ministry both as a pastor and as a missionary evangelist.

His massive frame dwarfed the pulpit as he began to speak of "praising God more, and repenting less." Not being interested in doing either one, I leaned over to my mother informing her of my intent to leave. She reminded me of our "deal" and obligated me to stick around for the rest of the show.

I crossed and uncrossed my legs, squirming in the pew, as he droned on about the importance of praising God in everyday life. The faithful affirmed him with "Amens" and "Praise God" as I sat imagining how smooth a snifter of Remy Martin would taste as soon as this fiasco was over.

"I don't know why I'm talking like this. This is not what I intended to preach on. The Holy Spirit must be directing me." Rev. Schoch seemed to have gone from zero to sixty in about ten seconds, stripping second and third gears while he cruised down the highway of the Spirit, now well on his way to breaking the speed limit.

"You must know the truth! You cannot live without truth! But truth is not a philosophy or a feeling—it is a person, and His name is Jesus Christ.

"You must know the truth! You cannot live without truth! But truth is not a philosophy or a feeling—it is a person, and His name is Jesus Christ. You may have heard about Him, read about Him, or listened to a preacher talk about Him, but if you have never had a personal encounter with Him, then you don't know Him and you have no truth!"

The magnitude of his words struck me in the core of my being. It felt like all eyes in the massive sanctuary were fixed like lasers peering into my soul. Suddenly my well-preserved, rock-like exterior, hardened by six years of self-promotion and abuse, was disintegrating. I tried frantically to hold my persona together, but each phrase out of the evangelist's mouth blasted away at the "great wall" that surrounded me everywhere I went.

"You need truth! You need Jesus! Jesus said, 'You will know *the* truth.' Not a truth, not some truth, THE truth. You will know THE truth, and THE truth will set you free."

As his words continued to flow, I could feel my security giving way. It was time to make my escape. Turning my head to gauge the distance between my location and the back door, my body was in the process of following my head as God's man issued an invitation.

It was too late now. I had missed my opportunity to make a break. Everyone now standing up, I decided to simply endure the usual altar call for people to go to the front of the church to pray and quietly leave during the closing prayer.

"If you want to *rededicate* your life to Jesus Christ, then I'm going to ask you to come down to the front. I want to pray with you."

The preacher's lingo was all too familiar to my jaded ears. Besides, how can you redo something you've never done in the first place? The organ hummed out a standard invitation hymn as Paul gave a second appeal.

"If you want to *recommit* your life to Jesus Christ, then come to the front."

Hadn't he realized that his "pitch" had no effect on me? The obvious impossibility of reenacting something never enacted made me safely exempt from having to respond to words I myself had used scores of times on just as many platforms.

Knowing he wouldn't want to "strike out" by issuing a third appeal, I was sure that my prison release was just one more chorus away. Anyway, he could feel secure in knowing that God had used him that evening, the altar area was full of respondents. I just didn't happen to be one of them.

The last word of the final song had been sung. Mentally, I was already speeding across Geary Street on the way to the Brazen Head for a nightcap.

"Danny! Come here in Jesus' name!"

The imaginary sports car came to a screeching halt as the brakes locked up in my mind. The audacity of the man to call me out publicly. Had he lost his mind? There was no way I was going up there. He could go straight to hell. My rage consumed my entire being as I thought of ways to make him pay for humiliating me.

"Danny," his index finger pointed in my direction, "I'm asking you to come down here right now, in the name of Jesus. Would you come?"

How many times in my life had I been "called out" in a service? Too many to remember. The last time was too long ago to recall. My dark curly hair shook from left to right as I registered my absolute refusal to yield to his invitation.

The cool facade was now replaced by a bone-chilling stare, as I tried to bore holes through his "breastplate of righteousness." Rev. Schoch held up the "shield of faith," deflecting the fiery darts that were being shot at him out of the depth of my demonized soul. The dimensions of my hatred for him and what he represented exceeded the bounds of any enmity I had ever known before.

All activity in the room seemed to stop as the prophet of God and I stood engaged in an invisible battle in the spirit realm that made Star Wars seem like child's play.

All activity in the room seemed to stop as the prophet of God and I stood engaged in an invisible battle in the spirit realm that made Star Wars seem like child's play. The angel hosts of the Living God were marshaled against the denizens of the domain of the Dark Prince, the diabolical spies being outnumbered two to one.

The strange-sounding language of the Spirit being quietly prayed by my mother struck my ears like a clarion call that harkened back to the days when she would intercede for me with hot tears and unknown tongues.

My countenance now revealed the magnitude of demonic possession that had been permitted to take the place of authority and dominion in my heart. Mom's spirit raced to the throne of God as she witnessed the shroud of darkness that was veiling her son's face.

Assured of present victory in the skirmish, I waited for the Reverend to concede defeat and relinquish the reins of the service back into the hands of Pastor Johnson, the present minister at Glad Tidings, so he could close the meeting.

Melvin Johnson was one of the gentlest men I had ever met. Shortly after he assumed the pastorate at the temple, he had called me with a lunch invitation. I accepted, wondering why he would want to spend any time with me.

We enjoyed a rather pleasant afternoon as I explained the details of my life to him. The posh outdoor bistro on upscale Union Street was an adequate setting for our repartee. The gracious minister, even managing to appear unaffected by the cigarette smoke that billowed out of my mouth as I talked, gave me his undivided attention and seemed genuinely interested in my story. I thanked him for his interest and the invitation and went on my way, thinking that our paths would never cross again.

The thrill of victory washed out of me as Evangelist Schoch descended the platform and began to make his way, with bulldog tenacity, up the aisle. The sight of him coming toward me elevated my rage as I attempted to stare him back to where he came from.

"Danny, God loves you and wants you to give Him your life." His arm, which felt like the limb of an oak tree, was now draped across my shoulders.

"Danny, God loves you and wants you to give Him your life." His arm, which felt like the limb of an oak tree, was now draped across my shoulders. I had been unable to make him retreat. I knew the scripture that bolstered his holy boldness, "Greater is he that is in you, than he who is in the world." I was on the losing end of that proposition.

"Get away from me… leave me alone. I don't believe in God! You're wasting your breath. He doesn't exist…He's not even real." Surely, he would leave me alone now.

"Danny, proof of the fact that God exists and that He is real is that you're standing here tonight. You should be dead. Many times your life has been spared. The devil has tried to destroy you in many ways, but God's mercy has kept you. His hand has been on your life all these years."

How could he know those things? The recognition of the gift of the Holy Spirit, known as the Word of Knowledge, was undeniable. My insides began to tremble as the manifestation of God's power began to be released through a modern-day Elisha.

"Danny, would you go to the altar with me? I want to pray for you." His plea was non-threatening. After all, I had been prayed over by some of the "biggest names in the business." Surely this would come and go without incident.

As we made our way to the altar, whispers of "Jesus, Jesus" could be heard coming from the crowd of intercessors. The sight of these two travelers, one blanketed in blackness and the other robed in shining light, filled the sanctuary with a heightened anticipation that recalled the days gone-by when lost sinners looked to Glad Tidings Temple as the beacon in the darkness.

Paul Schoch placed both hands on my head and began to pray for my deliverance. Suddenly, without notice, he moved a few feet away and left me abandoned. The thought running through my mind was that surely a militia of prayer warriors would descend upon me and finish the job. It was definitely time to leave.

The spiritual SWAT team never materialized, but God's servant was standing at my side once again. The same hands were laid on my head, this time as conduits of the power of God.

As he engaged the forces of darkness in conflict, my knees gave way placing me in a position that I hadn't been in for six years. The sounds of "church folk" crying out to God for mercy to be shown to me filled my hearing.

Sister Schoch, Paul's saintly spouse, was overcome by the Holy Spirit as she lay prostrate on the front pew, a few feet behind me. The gut-wrenching groans coming from within her being revealed an intensity of intercessory ministry that she had never experienced before. It was as though she were in labor, straining with every spiritual muscle she possessed to make sure that there would be a successful delivery.

My spirit, soul, and body were in crisis. I couldn't go back. I'd come too far now. It was too late to get up and walk out, and I didn't think I could even if I wanted to. I had reached an impasse, not knowing how to cross over to the place where the rest of the church was.

Was I really a "sinner?" Not having ever experienced the convicting power of the Holy Spirit in my life left me at a loss to identify my spiritual condition. Silently, my soul asked for a revelation of my lost state.

The crowd noise mysteriously became a distant backdrop to the images that were appearing on my mental screen. The Schochs' sounds lingered somewhere in the atmosphere while I became cognizant of nothing except the first-run, technicolor production I was now viewing.

A midnight sky hung overhead, while the one street lamp illuminated the city block, providing enough visibility to the see the sidewalk. The asphalt shone as though a winter rain had just stopped falling. There was no movement or activity on the street of any kind. Just then, out of my peripheral vision, from the left side of the street, I caught sight of a four-footed beast of unidentifiable species making his way along the sidewalk.

As the creature moved into range, the blackness of his fur glistened from having been a victim of the storm. Each one of his massive paws revealed threatening claws that looked as though they would scar the concrete walkway as he slinked further down the street.

Desperately wanting to see this animal's face, I cautiously moved out ahead of him and crossed the street so as to be in a position to view him head on, but far enough away to be out of harm's way.

My vantage point was now the most opportune—I focused on him, a sense of exhilaration mixed with trepidation underlying my anticipation. His head was turning in my direction, I could almost see his facial markings...he looked like...me!

The surround sound was suddenly deafening as the screen rolled up with a snap. The movie was over, and I was back to reality. *My God, that's what I really am—a wild animal living in the midst of darkness. I am vile, wretched. I am altogether darkness...I really am a sinner.*

"God, help me. Please, help me." The cries in my soul were so loud that I was sure they could be heard outside my body.

At that very moment, Brother Schoch encouraged me, "Danny,

just call on Jesus,. Say, 'Jesus, Jesus.'"

The prospect of calling upon that name filled me with expectation and hope. The tip of my tongue found the ridge of the roof of my mouth, while my lips parted to release the only name that could set me free.

But the wind needed to speak the name caught in my throat. Trying again, I repeated the process, but the same resistance was present, forbidding me to call upon the name that is above every other name.

Again and again I tried, but to no avail. I knew that the years of darkness, living in submission to the prince of this world, had rendered me powerless to help myself now that I desperately wanted it.

From the inner regions of my soul, my inner man began to confess the Christ . . .

From the inner regions of my soul, my inner man began to confess the Christ..."You are the Son of God. You died for my sins and shed Your precious blood on the cross of Calvary for me. You are the spotless Lamb of God. I repent of my sins...please forgive me. I turn from the world, the devil and my own sinful life, and I turn to You. I accept You and receive You as my Savior. Oh..."

His name resounded throughout the sanctuary as I was released to cry out to my Deliverer. "Jesus, Jesus, Jesus"—with every utterance of His name, another chain was broken off of my life. Praying onlookers witnessed my behavior as I, without realizing my actions, grabbed hold of invisible chains and ripped them from my body with every declaration of His name.

Unable to prevent the stream of syllables that formed the sweetest name sung by men and angels, I spoke the name, that for years had been an expression of my anger and bitterness, now, as the hymn writer penned, the sweetest name I know.

The sentence of death had been lifted, the guilty verdict was overturned and I was declared INNOCENT!

In hushed tones I cried out for cleansing. The years of abuse and self-gratification had taken me through portals of decadence and licentiousness, the residue of which was still present in my system.

"Jesus, I know about Your blood. I preached about Your blood, and sang of Your blood, but I've never known the cleansing power of Your blood. Please, Jesus, cleanse me and wash me with Your precious blood."

The pulsating rush of divine plasma circulated throughout the arteries and veins of my body, engulfing and swallowing up the contaminated, diseased serum of my wasted life. This experience was so real that it was necessary to look at the veins in my wrist for I was absolutely sure that I would be able to visibly view the flowing of the cleansing stream.

For the first time in my life I knew the reality of the hymn pronouncing Christ's atonement, which I had sung countless times as a child:

"There is a fountain filled with blood, drawn from Immanuel's veins,
And sinners plunged beneath that flood, lose all their guilty stains."

How was it possible to be transformed in a moment's time from feeling like the inside of a trash can to a hand-blown crystal vase, pristine and ready for the Master's use.

What can wash away my sins? NOTHING but the blood of Jesus!
What can make me whole again? NOTHING but the blood of Jesus!
Oh precious is the flow that makes me white as snow.
No other fount I know. NOTHING but the blood of Jesus!

There was no salvo known to man that was able to produce the change in my soul. No agent of cleansing had ever been invented that could expunge every crimson stain that permeated and fixed itself to the fiber of man's being. Nothing but the blood of the Lamb.

Cleansed, washed, purified...there weren't enough words in the English language to adequately describe what had happened.

The power that had served as my source of strength was now vanquished. No longer would I depend on diabolical dynamism to bolster my self-image. It was immediately evident to me that I would have to possess an inner power in order to live the life that I had just confessed.

> **"Oh Lord, I need Your power in my life. I must be filled with the power of the Holy Spirit or I cannot live for You."**

A quiet request for divine energy went straight to the throne. "Oh Lord, I need Your power in my life. I must be filled with the power of the Holy Spirit or I cannot live for You. Please fill me to overflowing with that power, just like You said would happen in the book of Acts. I want to be filled with power from on high."

The response from heaven was automatic. Within the depths of my existence, the epicenter of my innermost being had been awakened, as invisible floodwaters began to rise. The deluge was reaching flood stage, my spirit-man reeling with unspeakable joy as the reality of His presence caused me to know that I was actually, finally seated with Christ in heavenly places.

Living water, yes. Water that was really alive within me surged past the banks of my vocal chords and swirled like a whirlpool in my mouth. *If I don't open my mouth and let this out, I'm going to choke. I can't hold it in any longer!*

Syllables became words joined together in phrases that defied etymology. The torrent of the life-giving stream manifested in a linguistic expression that cannot be learned nor taught. It was a glorious, precious, marvelous gift that was granted to me that night. It seemed as though it would never stop.

All of my adoration and gratitude to the Lord of glory was being transmitted through the voice of Pentecost, imparting to me a mode of Holy Spirit-energized communication that could not be scrutinized, denied, or theologized out of existence. It was too late now. I had gotten a taste of the real deal.

Now cleansed from the past, filled with power for the present, there remained two items of business that needed attending to before I could be released from my place of surrender at the altar.

Praying a silent prayer heard by no one but the Lord, I had to know why my life had taken the path that it had. "Why didn't I know You? I was able to bring other people to You, but I never knew You."

Indeed, the scores of individuals who had given their lives to Jesus Christ experienced the reality of salvation through my preaching, but if Jesus had returned for the church at the close of any one of those altar calls, the "saved" would have gone with Him, and I would have been left on the platform, grasping a now useless pulpit.

"Was I some type of experiment that you were conducting? Called, gifted, and anointed without the knowledge of the Christ in my life. Why couldn't I know You the way everyone else did? Why did my search last so long and go on without discovery until tonight? Before I get up off my knees I have to know."

As soon as my spirit said an "Amen" to my silent request, a spontaneous communiqué in the language of 1 Corinthians 12 was uttered by someone in the congregation. That spirit of intercession made contact with the mercy seat in the Most Holy Place, followed by an immediate reply in plain English through Prophet Schoch.

"My son, I have always longed for you to know Me. I have reached out to you throughout the years of your life in order to reveal myself to you. The reason you never knew Me is because there was never room for Me in your life. I am not a tenant. I am not a renter. I am the landlord. When I enter a life, I enter to take control and ownership. You wanted to keep me in the lobby of your existence. I am the owner, and the manager. You were never willing to give Me total control of your life, and I will not go where I do not have control. But tonight you have been made ready, and I have revealed myself to you, and you will know Me, whom to know is life eternal. Thus saith the Lord."

The revolutionary words of the Catholic priest, spoken to me in the confessional, reverberated in my mind. "My son, when you're ready, God will find you."

"Lord, could I ask one more thing? I desperately need to know if You can still use me. My life has really been messed up, and I don't know what to do now. There are so many loose ends that need tying and my past is pretty ugly. Do you still have a plan for me? Is there still something that I can do? Can You use me again?"

The last silent question had been spoken by my now-regenerated, neophyte soul. With precision accuracy, the message came this time through another vessel in the crowd. Prophetic grace manifested once more through the servant of the Lord who had stayed by my broken side over the last hour, pouring on the oil and the wine.

"My son, the same call that I placed upon your life in your mother's womb is still in effect. I have not changed My mind concerning you. I still have a plan for you...I will use you again, but this time your ministry will operate out of relationship with Me. I am going to use you for My glory, and not your own. The same call and gifting are resident within you, and I will anoint you afresh for My service. Trust Me with all of your ways, seek My face every day, and I will raise you up from that place of revelation to do My will, says the Lord."

The darkness of the evening no longer held the ominous portent of destruction that I had been all too familiar with over the last six years. Walking to my car, I sensed the presence of angels who had been given a new assignment. The tears hadn't stopped since I had left the altar and the sounds of "Thank You, Jesus," replaced the usually melancholy sounds of the night coming from my cassette player, as I drove home.

Chapter Ten

Carried by the Wind

Marian, can you come over to my place? I need to talk to you. Something happened to me last night, and I want to tell you about it."

Sure that I was up to something and not believing me for a second, Marian arrived at my house a few minutes later.

"You're not serious. You're joking, right? You? Saved? I don't believe you."

I couldn't blame her. She had been witness to my life in the fast lane for the last three years. She knew how vehemently opposed I was to anything having to do with "church." I had made the declaration to her numerous times that I would never go back, nor would I ever be in the ministry again.

Hours later, the details of the evening of Tuesday, February 15, 1983, now all revealed, Marian accepted the fact that I had been "born again." I don't think I looked any different, but I knew that I was. It had been a thirty-two-year-long journey, but I was finally home.

Now what? It was apparent that the club scene was going to be a thing of the past. I could feel the vestiges of the old Danny trying to maintain their place in my life, while my new nature was giving them their eviction notice.

Some weeks after my conversion, my connection to Casanova's came to an end. I knew that I had to walk away from it, even if it meant being unemployed for a while. It was time to begin trusting the Lord in all of my ways.

The Lord lent his assistance in aiding my departure by sending a rainstorm into the San Francisco area that all but obliterated most of the night spot business in the area. It went on record as one of the worst storms in the city's history. No coincidence, as I found out later, that there was a Spanish Pentecostal church four doors away from the club that had been praying for the Lord to shut us down.

A door opened in the radio advertising business, and I took a position as local sales manager, working out of my home office, for a station in San Jose. It was exactly what I needed to bring my life into some sense of order and normalcy.

Pastor Johnson became a part of that order and normalcy as I began to make my way back to the church that I had known the better part of my life. His caring, mentoring ways drew me into a warm place that protected me from whatever criticism I might have encountered from some of the church folks who "knew me when."

It wasn't an every Sunday experience in the beginning. My usual Sunday morning routine had been to wake up close to noon, after having been up the night before till all hours of the morning, fumble for a cigarette and glance at the Sunday paper, while making an eye-opening cup of Bustelo Cuban coffee.

Marian had dropped out of the church a couple of years before, tired of the hypocrisy and ho-hum religion that she had known growing up, so initially whether or not I went wasn't an issue with her.

Time passed, and my commitment to the Lord and to Marian grew in intensity and devotion.

Time passed, and my commitment to the Lord and to Marian grew in intensity and devotion. Knowing that this was the will of the Lord for my life, Marian Garcia and I were married in the early part of that same year.

We began attending church together, she reluctantly at first. Having been raised in a conservative Spanish Southern Baptist church, the prospect of being comfortable in a Pentecostal setting was not immediately appealing.

Slowly but surely, the Lord began the lifelong process of conforming me to his image. Sunday morning attendance soon became Sunday and midweek evening service as I took my place on the Potter's Wheel.

Nearly a year after the grace of the Lord had been shed abroad in my heart, my pastor asked me if I would like to give my testimony in church. I hadn't so much as said a hearty "amen" publicly, during those first eleven months.

Pastor Johnson scheduled me to speak at the Sunday afternoon service. As the events of my life unfolded in that room, the Holy Spirit began speaking to hearts, urging hearers to come into a deeper relationship with the Lord.

Soon after, doors opened for me to share my story in other places. Marian and I began singing together, she the accomplished vocalist and me the harmonizing student under her tutelage. But the Lord had placed a powerful anointing upon our ministry that superceded my lack of professional vocal training.

The Lord began reviving the call to ministry in that following year. By this time, our son Santino had arrived, bringing with him all the joy that anyone could ask for in a first child. How gracious the Lord had been to me already by allowing me to stand before the sacred desk once again, blessing me with a wonderful wife and a healthy, strong, and handsome son.

Trying to find opportunities to preach in churches wasn't as easy as I thought it would be. We had produced a brochure on our ministry and sent it out to about four hundred churches in the San Francisco Bay Area. It was professionally done, complete with tear-off reply card, and a reproducible promo picture.

I was sure that the post office box we had opened up would be stuffed to overflowing the next week with responses from pastors who were just dying to have us come to their churches. Trips to the post office were made daily, even twice a day sometimes, to retrieve the reply cards that were to be sent back.

I never knew a P.O. Box could look so empty. I thought, "Welcome to the real world of itinerant ministry beginnings." The double trouble twins of *doubt* and *discouragement* started to make visits to my mind and heart.

"God, I thought you called me." Days turned into weeks as I waited for at least one reply. Phone calls were made to some of the pastors that had received the mailer. Trying to talk to some of them was more difficult than trying to reach the CEO of a Fortune 500 company.

While in study and prayer one morning, God spoke to my heart and indicated that there were forty cities in the Bay Area that I was going to minister in.

"Forty cities? I can't buy a service, and You're telling me I'm going to preach in forty cities?"

In total obedience, I listed them on a piece of paper and stuck it in the back of my study Bible, sure I would never have to look at that list again. Two weeks later, my usual post office routine now so familiar I could do it in my sleep, I made the trek to the brick building ready to leave it empty-handed once again. I was sure the postal workers were grateful to me for not having to reach up in the top row of boxes to place mail in Number 411322.

Preparing to slam the little square door shut for the thousandth time, I quickly turned the key to open and close the door as fast as possible so as not to have to peer into the empty cavern too long.

There, to my shock, was a single, tear-off reply card. "Was there a mistake? Surely one of them was sent back due to insufficient postage." No, a real pastor had actually taken the time to read the brochure, fill out the card, and send it back. "Lord, You really did call me!"

Setting new speed records for the distance from the post office to our apartment, my feet flew up the thirty-two stone stairs as I entered the hallway. "Honey, we got one!"

Marian met me in the hallway, Santino in her arms, to find out what the commotion was all about. "Look, a pastor in a place called Rohnert Park, sent it. I'm going to call him now!"

I didn't even know where Rohnert Park was, nor did I care. I just prayed that the pastor hadn't changed his mind in the meantime.

"Yes, I believe we have that Sunday open…just let me check my date book to make sure." Who was I kidding? That one Sunday was as available as the rest of the fifty-one others. "We'd love to come and minister in your church. Thank you for the invitation…we'll be there."

The scheduled Sunday came, and with it brought an evidence of the blessing of the Lord as Marian and I ministered in music and word. The manifestation of the Holy Spirit in the meeting was glorious as people were touched by His grace in visible ways.

> **The Lord began to touch lives from the choir loft to the back pew as the Holy Spirit swept through the many Sunday night services we had all over the San Francisco Bay Area.**

Meetings began to open up as pastors became acquainted with our ministry and the work of the Holy Spirit flowing through our lives. We began to witness miracles of healing and deliverance, along with the operation of the word of knowledge in the services. The Lord began to touch lives from the choir loft to the back pew as the Holy Spirit swept through the many Sunday night services we had all over the San Francisco Bay Area.

One Sunday night, closing out a weekend revival meeting in an East Bay church, a young lady came forward for prayer. She was even taller than I was and I had to reach up to lay hands on her. She "fell out under the power of the Holy Spirit," lying on the floor until the meeting was nearly over.

Retrieving my overcoat and Bible, I was startled by a shriek. Spinning around in the direction of the sound, I saw the girl who had been on the floor, now standing in disbelief at her condition.

"My feet, my feet...they're straight! The Lord has healed me." Her once severely turned in feet were now completely straight. I had to step over the abandoned corrective shoes left on the steps of the church, no longer usable, as I went to my car.

Substance abusers, preachers' kids, church board officials, choir members, the emotionally disfigured, and the spiritually hungry flooded the altars in church after church, twenty-five weekends a year.

My responsibilities as a husband and father increased as Gina, our baby girl, came two years after Santino. The sweetness of all that a daughter is supposed to be came into our lives in that adorable bundle.

Marian had gone back to college to study nursing, while I worked two jobs to put her through school and provide for our family. I was also ministering as a part of the staff at Glad Tidings, leading worship and working with the choir.

The desire to advance educationally brought me to the Bible Extension Institute of the Evangelical Church Alliance. After completion of a two-year program in Pastoral Theology, I was ordained to the ministry on an April Sunday morning in 1987.

The large hands of Rev. Paul Schoch rested on my head once again. But this time the purpose was not to declare spiritual authority against evil entities, but instead to officially recognize the oracle of the Lord that had been spoken before I was ever knit together in my mother's womb.

His hands were joined in ecclesiastical union with those of Pastor Melvin Johnson and Rev. Charles Wilson, a regional representative of the Evangelical Church Alliance. Leon Patillo had made a guest appearance, singing a song written for the occasion entitled *So Go Out and Bless the World.*

> **Open doors that no man could shut provided opportunities for the activity of the Holy Spirit in signs and wonders.**

The Lord's favor on the ministry continued as we ministered in denominational and independent churches of all varieties. Open doors that no man could shut provided opportunities for the activity of the Holy Spirit in signs and wonders.

One such opportunity found us at a large Assembly of God church in Richmond, California. After having shared my testimony in the evening service and having witnessed once again the power of the Holy Spirit in the lives of the people, a kindly saint approached me on the platform.

Stretching out his arm to greet me, he expressed his appreciation for what the Lord had done that night. There was something vaguely familiar about him, although I had no inkling of who he could be. My assumption was that he was a charter member of the church or a faithful board member. His hand still holding onto mine, he revealed his identity.

"Son, I am Ovid Dillingham."

A rush of tears filled my eyes as I realized that this was the same man who had prophesied over me for the first time in my life. I had no idea where he was or what had become of him after that first encounter. I had even mentioned his name and the experience in the giving of my testimony that night. It had been twenty-five years since the elder statesman had declared the will of the Lord concerning me, and now he and I had been privileged to see with our own eyes the faithfulness of the Lord. He was now retired from the mission field and serving as a minister to the senior citizens in that church. We both rejoiced in knowing that He who calls you is faithful.

1989 brought blessing and hardship. On the very day that Marian was to graduate from nursing school, we buried her beloved father, who had modeled for her the picture of love, nurturing and protection that allowed her to have a closeness to and security in her Heavenly Father. Her graduation ceremony and celebration was bittersweet, knowing that it would have been Don Pedro Raphael Garcia's crowning glory to be able to sit among the proud onlookers as Marian received her degree.

The Lord had spoken to her and let her know that He would sustain her. Her strength was in knowing that her "Papa" had been crowned with eternal glory by the Lord of Glory at the moment his tired heart had ceased to beat a few days prior. She learned that day what it meant to dwell in the secret place of the Most High.

As the evangelistic ministry blossomed, more Sunday morning and evening meetings were added to our itinerary. Being present to serve at Glad Tidings was becoming less frequent. We had been out two weekends in a row and were back on the second Sunday in December.

Taking my place on the platform after having led in praise and worship, my eyes scanned the bulletin as the announcements were being given.

"Look at your name in the bulletin in the order of service...it will never be there again."

The resonance of that voice was unmistakable. I had learned to identify the timbre and the pattern of God's impressions upon my spirit. Trying to find some other rationale for what I had heard, including the possibility of having poorly digested a slice of pizza the night before, I was at a loss to understand what had just transpired. Three days later, following a Wednesday night service, my pastor asked to see me in his office.

"Danny, I have had to come to a decision. It wasn't an easy one, but God has indicated to me that I have to let you go. I can't explain it all, but I know that you will never be what God wants you to be as long as you remain here."

"But, Pastor, I'm happy here. I don't want to stop serving under you."

"I'm sorry, Danny. This is the way it has to be. God has spoken to me, and I have to obey him."

"Pastor, this has cut me deeply. I'm bleeding all over your floor." Tears of confusion and disappointment dripped onto my lips as I tried, in vain, to change his mind. "When is this going to happen?" I asked, sure that I would stay on till the end of the year.

"It's effective right now."

I had not heard his reply incorrectly, neither had I mistaken God's notice to me that previous Sunday morning. My name never appeared in the Sunday bulletin again.

"God, there must be a reason for all this," I cried out on my way home that evening. "I don't know if You prompted this, or if You simply allowed it, but whatever the case, I accept it."

1990 was the busiest year ever. Our schedule for 1991 was already booked in advance. A vacation seemed like just the thing we needed to relax and refresh as we headed to Lake Tahoe for a few days together as a family.

The serenity of the woods accompanied me as I lay awake in the night listening to the precious sounds of my little ones in the adjoining room, breathing out the exhaustion of a day at play. Marian, lying next to me, was enjoying the kind of sleep that can only be experienced in mountain air.

Drowsiness was finally starting to fall upon me as I heard the voice that thunders as well as whispers. The whisper was definite. "I am changing your agenda. When you get back home, you will need to cancel all of your scheduled meetings for next year. I am going to use you to raise up a new church. You will open the doors on January 6, 1991."

"Wait a minute," I remonstrated, "This evangelistic ministry is finally getting to the place where it's accepted by churches, and the bookings are no longer hard to come by. God, what is the purpose in all this?"

"Remember that I called you first as a pastor, when you were two and a half years old. There is still a need for churches that will not be afraid or ashamed of My power or the demonstration of My Spirit in healing, deliverance, and restoration of mind, body, and spirit."

No further explanation was necessary. As that year progressed, we made preparations to give birth to a new ministry, *Genesis Worship Center...a place of beginnings*. Part of that preparation involved canceling the Sunday morning meetings we had scheduled for the next year and rescheduling a number of Sunday nights. As I looked over our itinerary from the previous years, I realized that the promise of God had come to pass. In all of the places where we had been graciously allowed to minister, the forty cities that God had spoken to me about were among that listing.

Now there were only a few small obstacles. We had no congregation or place to meet. To make matters even more dubious, we had no idea where we should start. What we did have was a church name, a vision, and a mandate.

Buildings of every shape and size were investigated everywhere we went, from tiny storefronts to supermarkets that had long since gone out of business. Everything was either too small or too expensive for a church with no people and no money.

Days were turning into weeks and months as the January date drew closer. All of the legal requirements for incorporation had been attended to, equipment was being purchased little by little while Marian and I were preparing our hearts to enter into a field of service that neither one of us really wanted. What we did want was to please God, in whatever way He chose.

By the end of October, the anxiety was starting to become overwhelming. Driving across a set of railroad tracks in the industrial section of San Francisco one morning in particular, my frustration level had reached an all-time high.

I mean, at least the disciples knew they were going to begin in Jerusalem. What do You expect me to do?"

"God, you called me into this. I have no building. I don't even know where You want us to start. I mean, at least the disciples knew they were going to begin in Jerusalem. What do You expect me to do?"

Peering through the blinding tears welling up in my eyes, I looked south and then north to make sure there was no oncoming traffic as I made my way through the intersection. Situated on the northwest corner was a dilapidated, corrugated-steel warehouse. In foot-high letters, someone with a "graffiti ministry" had spray painted the words on the gray wall, TRUST JESUS. The tears became rivulets of submission while I moved across those tracks, telling God that I would not doubt Him. Surely, He would provide.

A gathering of Marian's family took us to Pacifica, a small coastal city about fifteen minutes south of San Francisco. As we approached our destination, I spotted a quaint church on an adjoining street.

"Huh...a Filipino Seventh Day Adventist Church. I wonder if they would rent to us. It would work out. They don't use it on Sundays. But who wants to start a church in Pacifica? After all, the place is so well known for the amount of fog it gets throughout the year that they even hold an annual street fair called The Fog Fest."

I didn't have many options open. None, as a matter of fact. "Maybe this is where God wants us to start," I thought. The first

Tuesday night in November found me in the boardroom of the little church, sharing the burden that God had placed upon my heart.

Having originally been told that the church elders didn't want to rent to anyone, but that they would give me a chance to talk with them, I simply believed that if this is where God wanted us, then He would have to open the door.

Thirty minutes later, the ten "yes" votes and the two "no's" brought the plan of God to a place of concrete assurance. That first Sunday in January of 1991 brought family members, well wishers, and the curious to the church doors. God's blessing on His work was apparent as the packed house swayed under the power of the Holy Spirit.

The exhilaration of the initial gathering carried us through the week in anticipation of what would take place the following Sunday. Knowing that the great attendance was due to the inauguration activity, there was no way of knowing who would return the next week.

Fifteen people, including my wife and two children, decided to make Genesis their church home. A far cry from the one hundred celebrants the previous Sunday, but it was what God had given us.

The trials and testing of pastoral ministry were largely unexpected. Being an associate and traveling as an evangelist was "a walk in the park" compared to the demands of being an undershepherd in the body of Christ. We learned early on that "sheep bite."

> **From the very first meeting until today, we have seen the provision and blessing of God and can say with the hymn writer, "Great Is Thy Faithfulness."**

But the blessings and joys of seeing lives changed for eternity far outweigh the challenges and disappointments that come with the territory. From the very first meeting until today, we have seen the provision and blessing of God and can say with the hymn writer, "Great Is Thy Faithfulness."

The blessings of heaven have fallen on our family in manifold ways. Marian's anointed piano artistry and vocal gifting have ushered us into the secret place in worship week after week. Santino took after his Dad, rocking the house with drumming skills well beyond his years. And Gina's blossoming voice touches the hearts of those in the pews whenever she ministers.

The prophetic calling and confirmation upon my life has not ceased. Over the years, God has allowed my path to cross with His servants who have traced His hand that rests on me. Among the many who have borne witness to the fellowship of the prophet is Dr. Rodney Howard-Browne, who recognized the call of God and was used to speak into my life and ministry an impartation of power and revelation. The words of the Apostle Paul are just as true today as they were when they were written, "...for God's gifts and his call are irrevocable" (Romans 11:29).

The wisest man who ever lived said that the pursuit of self-aggrandizement and earthly pleasure is, in the end, meaningless. Solomon called this a chasing after the wind. Literally translated from the Hebrew language, it means, *the anxious striving of the mind,* which he determined in one word of summation, as meaningless, (worthless).

There remains only one wind worth chasing after. He will not run from you, He will not elude you.

There remains only one *wind* worth chasing after. He will not run from you, He will not elude you. But, instead, He will allow you to encounter Him and He will, as Jesus said, "guide you into all truth."

The days ahead are filled with the extension and the expansion of the kingdom of God in my life, and it is with great excitement and expectation that I exist caught up in the jet stream of the Wind of His Spirit.

The message of this book is that God loves you and wants you to know and receive His love. People are separated from God until they respond to the message of the cross of Jesus Christ. God sent his son to die for you and pay the price for your sins. You can receive the love of God by asking Jesus Christ to enter your life and become your Savior and Lord. You can invite him to do that right now and he will. If you have made that decision and would like further instruction on how to live a new life, contact: Rev. Danny DiAngelo, Genesis Worship Center, 1600 Santa Lucia Avenue, San Bruno, CA 94066-4736

*Rev. Danny DiAngelo, his wife, Marian,
and their two children, Santino and Gina.*

If you would like to receive a catalog of Rev. DiAngelo's tape ministry or are
interested in having him come to your area, contact:

Rev. Danny DiAngelo
Genesis Worship Center
1600 Santa Lucia Avenue
San Bruno, CA 94066-4736
650-952-1194
Fax: 650-952-1195
Email: *genesisworshipcenter@juno.com*